UNSHACKLED

JANIE BURKETT

A ROAD TO FREEDOM
UNSHACKLED

FOREWORD BY SHANNON ETHRIDGE

TATE PUBLISHING
AND ENTERPRISES, LLC

Published by Tate Publishing & Enterprises, LLC
127 E. Trade Center Terrace | Mustang, Oklahoma 73064 USA
1.888.361.9473 | www.tatepublishing.com

Tate Publishing is committed to excellence in the publishing industry. The company reflects the philosophy established by the founders, based on Psalm 68:11,

"The Lord gave the word and great was the company of those who published it."

Book design copyright © 2012 by Tate Publishing, LLC. All rights reserved.
Cover design by Joel Uber
Interior design by Jomar Ouano

Published in the United States of America

ISBN: 978-1-62295-622-7
1. Memoir
2. Christian Inspirational
12.12.27

There is no pit so deep that God's grace is not deeper still.

—Corrie Ten Boom

SPECIAL ACKNOWLEDGMENTS

I wish to thank:

First of all I would like to thank my heavenly Father for delivering me from a life of drugs, alcohol, and a life in prison. Without Him, I would not be here to tell my story.

My parents for their unfailing love that never gave up on me and their prayers that brought me through the hardest times of my life.

My mother for her ideas, editing, and encouragement.

My dad for his wisdom, support, and for believing in me when I didn't believe in myself.

For my sisters' love and prayers for me.

To the San Antonio Teen Challenge for giving me the help and support I needed to become the woman that God called me to be.

Lee Desmond for her part in editing.

Jill Saigusa for her help in writing the first chapter.

Shannon Ethridge and the Blast Program for the tools to make my dreams of becoming a speaker and showing other's God's love a reality.

A special thanks to all the people of Church Fellowship International in Henderson, TX, for their love, prayers, and support.

To my attorney Robert C. Perkins, Jr. for fighting for me.

To Todd Hilton for his part in the beginning stages on this process.

To Bob Burk for his support.

To the Late Wayne Gillespie for his encouragement.

A special thanks to my wonderful husband, Jonathan Harrison, and his family for their love and support.

FOREWORD

When I met Janie Burkett in March 2010, she struck me as a woman *on fire*. An overwhelming passion for God oozed out of her pores, and I could see in her sparkling blue eyes that she was on a mission. I had no idea that I would soon become a part of God's plan in helping her fulfill that mission.

I was speaking at a Celebrate Recovery meeting at Green Acres Baptist Church, and toward the end of my talk, I mentioned the online BLAST Mentorship Program (Building Leaders, Authors, Speakers, and Teachers). After that session, Janie approached me wide-eyed, eager to learn more. I shared the basics of the one-year program with her, and she responded that she was very interested.

But there was this one big thing that she feared may disqualify her from participating. "I just got out of prison," Janie explained, assuming that I might, as a result, simply shake her hand good-bye and bid her farewell. "Can I still do BLAST?" she humbly asked.

After hearing more of the details about the tragedies in her life that led her into prison and the miracles that led her out, I said to her, "Janie, I don't think I can mentor you through the online program. I think I can do better."

Just three weeks prior to this divine encounter, my husband and I had made a decision to open our home to a handful of young women who wanted to serve in a residential internship with Shannon Ethridge Ministries. These women would live with us, work alongside us, learn the ministry ropes, be exposed to the ins and outs and ups and downs of the publishing industry, and hopefully be inspired to launch their own speaking platform in God's timing. I had no idea who these women would be when we designed this program, but just like in the movie *Field of Dreams*, I sensed God saying, "If you build it, they will come!"

Standing there talking to Janie, I knew without a doubt that *she* was one of the young women God had in mind when He laid this idea on our hearts. When I invited Janie to be the *first* residential intern, the look on her face would have made you think she'd just won the lottery! Checking to make sure this was really happening, she asked emphatically, "And you heard me say that I just got out of prison, right? And you still want me to come and live with you? And you'll mentor me personally?"

Within a matter of days, Janie's entire family was sitting in my living room, all of us basking in God's sovereignty over what had taken place…eagerly anticipating what God would continue to do—*in* us, *through* us, and *in spite* of us when necessary.

Little did I know that it was *I* who won the spiritual lottery the day I met Janie. Having the opportunity to sow seeds into her life and ministry has been such a tremendous blessing! I've never seen a woman so eager to offer God her "lemons" in trust that He could surely make "lemonade" out of them!

For six months, I witnessed Janie get up early and fervently seek the Lord in prayer as if her life depended on it. She read her Bible religiously, filled her room with worship music, and wrote extensively in her journal. She contributed to the ministry, the household, and the internship program with a servant's heart. She watched the BLAST videos with an insatiable hunger to learn and grow as a speaker, a writer, and a minister of the gospel of Jesus Christ. She began receiving more and more invitations to speak at churches, and she eagerly walked through every door that God opened, seizing every opportunity to share the absolutely amazing miracles that God had performed in her heart and life.

You're about to discover some of those miracles in the coming pages of this book, and my hope is that as you learn more about Janie's testimony and life lessons learned, you'll be as inspired by her as I have been…and that you'll be inspired to fall as deeply in love with our life-changing God as she has.

Warmly,
Shannon Ethridge, M.A.
Certified Life Coach, International Speaker
and Best-Selling Author of 19 books, including *The Every Woman's Battle* series and *The Fantasy Fallacy*
www.shannonethridge.com

CHAPTER ONE

CONCRETE WALLS

Lying on the floor of a four-foot-by-eight-foot cell, naked and in the fetal position, I wonder if I'm awake or asleep. This has to be a nightmare. Someone has thrown a thin, blue blanket over me, and I clutch at it for warmth. My body quivers from the cold. I look down at my hands and barely recognize them—they are the thin, waiflike hands of an old woman. The skin is almost translucent, the veins a deep indigo blue. They are the hands of a stranger, and I cannot stop them from shaking.

From the hallway outside, I hear screaming, the cries of inmates cursing at one another and yelling at nurses for medication. This must be what hell feels like. I close my eyes and try to escape, but a movie plays itself out inside my eyelids. I'm sitting in the back of a van, and it's still dark out; the clock on the dashboard reads 5:30 a.m. The fog in my head is as thick as the fog outside the car windows. I feel dizzy, disoriented, and confused.

There's an officer seated next to me, and I ask him where I am.

"You're in Houston," he replies coldly, "being transferred to Jester Four for evaluation."

"What's Jester Four?" I ask.

"It's the psych ward."

Slowly, my memory comes back to me—the hospital in Galveston, the medication given to me for detox and bulimia. It seems I have slept for days.

Headlights cut through the fog, and in the distance I see a large brick building surrounded by a barbed-wire fence. We pull through the gates and come to a stop so the prison guards can search our van. They direct us down a long driveway to the back of the prison, where we stop at two stainless steel doors.

One of the guards leads me in shackles to a little room where a female guard is waiting for me. She unlocks the handcuffs around my hands and ankles.

"Get undressed," she barks. "Strip search."

She stares smugly as I strip naked, her probing fingers invading every square inch of my body. They search everywhere—my mouth, ears, hair—even my private parts. I have been through a lot in my life, and this ranks as one of the most degrading experiences I've ever had. My cheeks grow hot with humiliation as I hunch there, naked and terrified.

I wonder what the guard is thinking as she treats me more like an object than a person in this concrete room. I wonder how I must look to her, my stomach concave, my ribcage protruding, and my eyes sunken and hollow on my colorless face. She calls a nurse who measures my height—five feet, seven inches—and then asks me to step on the scale. The scale screams back at me, "One hundred and ten pounds!"

The nurse drapes a blanket over my shoulders in a brief moment of compassion and leads me down a long, narrow hallway. The white concrete walls of my cell are littered with graffiti; the only amenities are made of cold stainless steel—a toilet, a sink, a bed.

I will remain here in this bleak and lonely place, naked, for seven days; after that, for three weeks this will be my entire life for twenty-three hours and fifty minutes every day. I can leave only to shower, ten minutes max. Even then, though, I am kept in a cage.

I hear the clink of the cell door closing, and harsh, cold reality comes to call. I lie on the blue concrete floor and rock myself gently, singing in a hushed whisper the only songs I can remember, hymns taught to me by my parents. The memory of the words and their music seem to soothe me like a blanket of another kind, a blanket called comfort. This blanket is my one thread of sanity. It is a lifeline, and I cling to it, though it is as tenuous as a spider's web.

My weary eyes look to the narrow window of my cell, and the sharp sunlight streaming through causes tears to gather in the corners of my eyes. I dream of flying through that opening, soaring high above the earth and these prison walls, leaving it all behind; my body ravaged by drugs, alcohol and bulimia, the soul I have drowned and suffocated with self-torture and self-doubt. If I could only leave this hallowed shell of a person behind and find the person I could be if given half a chance. But it is useless, and I know it. I wipe the tears from my eyes and stare down to see my trembling hands and feeble fingers. Freedom, if it exists for me ever again, lies in a land far away. There is only here, and there is only now. I am not going anywhere.

In the darkness, I grasp for the blanket that had been given to me and cry out to God. I was raised to believe in God, and I hope that my prayer will touch His heart. I cry out for help with what little strength I have left. I ask Him to send angels to comfort me. I know it's a long shot, but I'm cold and desperate. What I don't realize is that, miles away, God has awakened my parents, and they are praying for me, too.

Praying to God for any kind of relief, I begin to wonder how it is that I got to this place. This has become somewhat normal for me, but it is completely foreign at the same time. I was not raised to become this person. I know that I am not this person. The question that I'm left with, then, is where did this person come from? The answer, I know, isn't exactly simple, and it begins a very long time ago.

CHAPTER TWO

A CRIPPLED FAITH, A CRIPPLED ME

Many people who end up a victim to the revolving door syndrome of incarceration can tell you the origin of their problem stems from neglectful parents. I am not one of those people. My issues did begin at an early age, but they have always been a derivative of my own insecurities. I have, for almost as long as I can remember, been in a constant battle with me.

The problem with me is that I began believing lies at only eight years old, and, as soon as I began to buy into one lie, the enemy offered a slew of them seeing my weakness, and I bought into those as well. The battle that has been created from that original deception has led me down certain paths that have only amplified the demons that I have fought. To grasp the gravity of my situation, it is best to understand exactly all that I've been up against.

I was born in Paris, Texas, but raised in Valliant, Oklahoma, with my two sisters, Faith, who was three years older, and Rebekah, who was only fourteen months younger and my best friend. My parents, Dr. Leland and Jan Burkett, were pastors of the First Assembly of God Church, which was vibrant and growing and almost seemed out of place in such a small town with a population of approximately nine hundred. Our church had a large Family Life Center that was a hub of activity for the tiny little town of Valliant. Within the church, our family had built a good life and established countless close friendships. There was a comfort that I found within my large church family; however, my biggest source of happiness came from being with my sister Rebekah.

Rebekah and I did everything together. I remember how much fun we had making mud pies, swimming in our kiddy pool, and playing dolls. We even slept in the same bed for years. To say that we were close doesn't even touch it. We had our differences, though; she was pretty and petite, and I was cute and chubby, but we never noticed the differences. We complemented one another perfectly, and, as far as we could tell, we were complete equals.

Rebekah and I both had beautiful voices and loved to sing. When I was eight and Rebekah seven, our parents let us enter a school talent competition. This was an exciting event for both of us. We would both get the opportunity to share something we were proud of: our voices. What we failed to realize in the excitement of entering the contest was that we would be competing against one another. Suddenly, sibling rivalry was introduced into our perfect relationship of sisterhood and friendship.

The day of the competition arrived, and the results would begin to mold my self-image from that day forward. Rebekah won first place, and I won second. I became conscious of something that would slowly unravel all that had kept me together; Rebekah and I were not equals. I cried for weeks. I was never the same.

A disturbing new self-consciousness crept into the core of my being, and I began to feel inadequate, not only to her but to everyone around me. In my mind, I was not good enough for anything or anyone; my insecurities and the fear of failing was replacing the happiness and confidence I once had. The strength and comfort I had found in my little sister had been choked out by the weeds of self-doubt and jealousy, and my safe haven was beginning to collapse. At only eight years old, I had begun to conquer myself.

I began to eat in an attempt to comfort myself, which only created more problems for me. I had always been a cute, chubby little girl; I had an adorably round face that was framed by golden curls and had a tiny "beauty mark" on the side of my nose. With a smile always on my plump face, I was the picture of sweetness, but slowly I felt that the "cute" was slipping, and I was left as just a chubby little girl. There were plenty of people around me to reinforce that notion, too.

I started to be bullied, and some of the more cruel kids at school would go so far as to call me Miss Piggy; the blond curls and beauty mark had suddenly become a liability instead of an asset. I withdrew and became quiet and severely insecure. I couldn't understand what I had done to have so much pain inflicted upon me. I had, up to that point, been an outgoing little girl with a drive to help anyone who needed it. I wanted nothing more than to show anyone I could God's love. I was on fire for the Lord and I wanted everyone else to truly know God's love, so I did my very best to show them. I had a passion for God and all His creation. I knew I had a calling on my life, and I had every intention of answering God's call in any way I could. It seemed I was being punished now, though, and I could not figure out my crime.

At that point, I realized that my body was a burden, and I began to hate everything about it, which led to hating everything about me. As self-doubt and self-consciousness overshadowed my confidence and love for life, my life seemed to be changing rapidly. The unbreakable bond I shared with my sister had suffered an irreparable blow, school had became a daily nightmare, my body felt more like a prison sentence every day, and that was just the beginning….

Our home revolved around the church. My dad devoted his life to God and to the church, while my mom was busy taking care of us and her many activities in the church. They were always busy "doing God's work," and God's work is no simple task. Both being ministers, my parents' daily lives involved pouring their hearts and souls into giving out spiritual food and attending to the needs of the congregation. Something that requires so much can be emotionally and spiritually draining. There were always counseling sessions, hospital calls, visitations, and so on. Such a lifestyle is undoubtedly a fulfilling one but also one that guarantees a lot of stress. Carrying the burden of so many people, it's only a matter of time before a person hits a wall of emotional exhaustion and, sometimes, a feeling of hopelessness.

If you're not careful, you can give more out emotionally, physically, and spiritually than you take in. I think that's what happened to my parents. They were giving so much of themselves to everyone else that they failed to retreat and spend time with one another and with God. It seems like a strange thing to say, but you can get so caught up working *for* God that you neglect your relationship *with* Him. My parents were helping families throughout our church set their own solid foundations and repair that which needed mending. In their quest to ensure the stability of other families' well-being, however, they began to drift apart from one another, and their marriage took a direct hit from the devil.

In August of 1994, my dad asked my mom for a divorce. She was devastated. My sisters and I were also heartbroken. They had been married sixteen years. Our home, our security, our lives, everything we knew rested on the foundation of our parents' marriage. They were the center that we revolved around, the constant that kept our worlds in check. We all lost our footing. The stability that we had began to crumble.

My sisters and I were not the only ones who took my parents splitting hard. The people of our church were stunned. Like our own family, the congregation had grown to depend on my parents for their own sense of security. Without my parents there to guide them, the flock had lost its shepherd. Unrest and strife started in our church. Rumors were circulating around the church, community, and even in our school. We were the talk of the town.

As ministers, people expect more of you. No decision you make is yours alone, no mistake you make is lightly taken, and you certainly are not allowed to experience a life-altering event privately. Your life is a twenty-four-hour program for those around you and you don't get to say "enough" when you're ready to opt out of the contract. Everyone is watching, and they are expecting more from you than they do from Jim next door or even from themselves. Sometimes people forget that ministers are human and they can make mistakes like anyone else—that they go through the same battles that everyone else does.

My parents decided to separate and take a sixty-day leave of absence from the church. The first month they went their separate ways. The second month they sought counseling and tried to work through their problems. The process wasn't easy for anyone, and it was affecting our church in a very real way. My mom and dad had been in the church for sixteen years, ever since they married. The people loved both of them and had a hard time accepting the separation of my parents. The entire congregation became the children of a breaking home. The church reacted in the very same way that children of divorcing parents might, and they began to choose sides.

Without any control of what was happening in the wake of their personal decisions, my parents' separation swelled beyond the walls of our home and created a split within our church. Some even left our church and abandoned my family. This was the next blow to my sense of security. By ten, I had begun to harbor bitterness and hatred as I watched family friends who had claimed to care for us disappear just as my world was being turned upside down.

The people that I had grown to love and respect had broken my heart. I couldn't understand why they would abandon us when we needed them most. We needed them to stand with us, pray for us, and ask God to restore our family. Instead, they chose to walk away. I became angry with my parents for separating, the church for turning their backs on us, and, most importantly, God for letting it all happen. The seed of hatred had been planted, and when watered with the rains of my insecurity, it sprouted and grew quickly. I hadn't even reached my teens yet, and I was harboring enough ill will to take down a small village.

CHAPTER THREE

LIFE ON THE ROAD

My mom and dad ultimately decided to stay together and try to work through their struggles. My dad broke down and told my mom that God had called him to be an evangelist years ago, but he had never told her. At first, my mom rejected the idea. Our father was not about to drag his family around the country from church to church. God began to speak to my mom about obeying the call of evangelism, though, and she finally gave in.

Soon my dad was calling his friends who were pastors to see if he could book a revival with them. They were completely booked. One pastor scheduled a revival, but it was six months away. It was harder than we thought. My dad is an awesome preacher, but the doors were not opening. God kept telling my dad to step out in faith, resign from the church, and obey Him, though, regardless of how things appeared. The Holy

Spirit told my mom to step out first and watch God perform a miracle, and that's what happened.

In July of 1995, my father stepped out in faith and resigned from the church with only one revival scheduled six months down the road. After thirty days, my dad preached his farewell message to the church. We were all in tears, but we knew our time in Valliant, Oklahoma, was over. Within a month, God blessed us with a motor home and our first revival. Out of that revival we got three immediate revivals and so on, and that's how God started us in a new season of life. The next five years of my life were spent on the evangelistic field going from one revival to the next. My dad went on to preach weeks at a time without ever having to wonder where he would go next. God would continue to provide.

I was eleven years old when we packed up and headed for cities unknown. It wasn't easy on the evangelistic field. There were five of us and our dog living in a twenty-eight-foot motor home. Living in tight quarters can be trying in short spans, and this was our daily life for years. The four of us women had to share a closet that was about three and a half feet by five feet. I will not compare my stories with Job's here, but I will say it was quite a challenge. Rebekah and I shared a table that turned into a bed, Faith slept in the pull down above the driver's seat, and Mom and Dad had a bed in the back.

There we were, living in this ridiculously small motor home with little room to move around. I was miserable. I have always been a homebody, and I missed our house and friends. I didn't understand why God would call us to do something that was so unpleasant for such a long period of time. My comfort zone was not a very big place, and this was certainly not a part of it.

Another thing that proved difficult for me was home school. Because we were constantly moving, my mom had to home school us. I had a learning disability, so it was much harder for me than it may have been for the average preteen. It couldn't have been easy for my mom, either, helping three girls at three different grade levels as we traveled around the country. Everyone's lives were drastically altered.

It was school during the day and church at night. We had to learn a new way of life that centered around constant change, and I was not a fan of change. My insecurities began to mount at this point. I relied on eating more than ever to deal with everything that was going on around me. Food became my coping mechanism, and that didn't bode well for a little girl who was already struggling with her weight. Food was there, though, and it offered what no one else seemed to at the time: comfort.

My dependence on food only grew as time passed. I began to realize that people were only temporary in my life. Food, however, was a constant, and I needed consistency somewhere. The only thing certain about my life was that I would have to say good-bye to anyone I had gotten close to in the new places we went. The hardest part, though, wasn't saying good-bye; it was the empty promises that the friends I made offered me as we left. I would make a friend and feel a real connection. We would both promise to write and talk on the phone when we could, but when we left, they were gone. I began to feel very forgettable. All I wanted was someone who thought I was worth the time and effort, but with each new town and each new prospective new friend, I was let down again and again. This made traveling especially difficult for me. I couldn't see the blessing that God was pouring on my family or the opportunity that God presented in all the new people my parents were able to touch. Because I had become so insecure and needed so much for someone to validate me, all I could see were people vanishing in the rearview mirror and friends turning to strangers.

As I fought with accepting myself and the situation I was in, something else began to happen that I had no idea would have such an impact on my life for such a long time. At twelve, I started having stomach problems that we couldn't figure out. I felt sick constantly. What we eventually found out was lactose intolerance introduced me to a monster named Bulimia. It wasn't an intentional meeting, though. Before I realized what was causing me to feel so bad all the time, I would make myself vomit to relieve my nausea. This went on for a short amount of time until the problem was finally diagnosed. I never did this with the specific purpose of losing weight, but I did notice that I had shed a few pounds during the process. Although bulimia wasn't something that I threw myself into at this time, it did sneak its way into a cracked door, and it lay waiting for the opportunity to throw that door open.

It is amazing how much a person can change over a five-year span of time, especially when the span covers adolescence to young adulthood. I was becoming a young woman as we traveled from town to town, and as I left my little girl habits of playing with dolls and making mud pies behind me, I began to pick up some bad habits to replace the old. As I worked my way into my middle teen years, I began to experiment with alcohol, and boys became a focal point. I tagged along with my older sister to parties and found a new place to hide my pain in a lifestyle that would, ironically, only create more confusion and hurt. I didn't think about consequences, though. I found a circuit that helped me forget a little about the things that I was tirelessly running from. Something happened in February of 2000 that would inflame everything that I was attempting to escape, though.

My family and I were in Houston, Texas, while my dad preached a revival. Faith and I, who had both been led astray by the party scene, were at the mall just killing time one evening when we met two guys. They told us their names, Bryant and James, and we told them ours. We sat and talked awhile; then they invited us back to their place. I immediately felt a little uneasy about going to a couple of guys' house after only knowing them for half an hour, but Faith felt comfortable with it, and at that point I would follow her into the pits of hell, so I went.

We got to Bryant and James's, and they offered us drinks, which we took. We sat around drinking for a bit; then my sister disappeared with Bryant. James and I were left in the living room alone. Suddenly, every fiber of being was pulling at me to leave. I knew by instinct that I was not in a good place, that nothing good was going to come from this situation.

I felt panicked sitting there alone with this guy whose last name I didn't even know. I felt panicked for a reason.

James began to force himself on me. As I resisted, he became more persistent. I kept repeating, "No, no, no," but he didn't care what I wanted at that point. In a stranger's living room in Houston, Texas, a man I would never see again raped me. I had felt the ultimate violation. The floodgates of my insecurities swung open, and everything I was trying to bury deep down inside me was pushed to the surface.

When it was over, I burst into the room my sister was in and screamed, "We've got to go, Faith. Now!" She had no idea what had happened or why I was so frantic; she could tell that I was serious, though, so she rushed to gather her things and get out of that apartment.

I was humiliated, ashamed, and outraged. I told myself that I must have caused it somehow, that it was my fault or I blamed my sister for not protecting me when I felt she should have. It wasn't her fault, though, and it wasn't mine either. Faith had no clue what was happening in the next room. Both the guys seemed nice enough from the beginning. She couldn't have known what would happen and still didn't after the fact because I didn't tell her. I only became angry with her because I needed to be angry with someone, and Faith was convenient. At the end of the day, though, I had no right to be mad at my big sister because she did not cause me to feel this way. James did. It was James who had violated me and caused this pain.

I was completely ashamed of myself and my body, which began to feel even more repulsive to me than it had before. Because I couldn't see that I was a victim of something horrific, I bore the cross for he who had sinned against me. Any bit of self-worth I had was gone.

Suddenly, I needed to have control over my body somehow to take back what had been stolen from me. I needed to do something that would make me feel less disgusted with myself. I had struggled with my body for so long because of my weight, and now something more horrible had come along to make everything worse. Searching for a respite, I remembered being twelve and purging. I remembered how I lost weight in the small amount of time that I did it. Most of all, I remembered how I was in control of myself when I would purge. Bulimia was now making its way to the forefront of my life. It would soon become my false idol. I had been sitting on the verge of disaster for quite some time, and having my body violated in such a violent way pushed me over the edge.

After being raped, I became so bitter that the change was unmistakable. My parents, of course, did not know what had happened, so they couldn't help me. There was but One I could've taken such a torment to, but I was now holding a grudge, so I had to deal with it on my own. I wasn't equipped at fifteen to deal with something so massive on my own, though; nobody is equipped to deal with something so massive on their own. I did the only thing I could think of to ease my pain and immersed myself into an eating disorder in an attempt to gain control.

I was full of hate and slowly turning my back on God, so self-destruction looked like my only choice. As far as I could tell, God wasn't doing me any favors, so He and I were not on speaking terms. My heart had hardened.

I got so lost while we were on the evangelistic field that I could no longer see God's hand in everything. I didn't want to see God's hand in everything yet; I wanted to be angry because nothing was going the way I wanted. I know now that it was a journey of faith for my dad and mom, but I was a young girl with a myriad of insecurities, and I resented my parents for dragging us along with them. It wasn't me that God had called, after all…right?

CHAPTER FOUR

PUTTING ON THE MASK

Just months after that horrible event, we settled down. My family had traveled from town to town preaching God's Word until finally in April 2000, when my family settled in Henderson, Texas. My dad started his own church in Henderson. At last, we had a place to call home. I began to fall into daily routines like everyone else with normal, everyday lives. As we laid down our roots and finally had a home address, I should have been on the brink of becoming complete.

There would be no new faces staring back at me like I was in an exhibit placed between the chimpanzees and the giraffes, no new towns from week to week to readjust to, to reintroduce myself to, or to walk away from. Things were finally settling down, so my troubles should have been behind me. There was only one detail nagging me, one thing that was separating me from the happiness I sought: nothing was really better. In fact, things seemed to be getting worse. I still had my past, I was now fifteen and tipping the scales at close to 200 pounds, and my eating disorder was gaining steam. Most importantly, I still had a beef with God.

My insecurities were all encompassing; they were drowning out everything else about me. As my self-image issues swelled, I leaned more and more on all the wrong things to keep them at bay. At sixteen, I began working as a server in a restaurant. I noticed how the men that came in paid attention to me, and I liked the feeling. I have always been a flirtatious person, and I had really started to come into my own at this point—my own private hell.

Now that we were settled, I had no idea what to do with myself. I had become so accustomed to constantly moving that I had no idea how to stay still anymore. I had to find something to keep me going; I didn't want to become stagnant in the little town of Henderson. I finally decided that partying would be the answer to all my problems. I wouldn't have to be still, wouldn't have to be alone, and, most importantly, I wouldn't have to deal with any of my problems.

As I was slipping further into a life that promised only hurt and pain, my parents were praying and fighting for me every step of the way. They could see that they were losing me. My mom and dad both would sit me down and talk to me about my life and what was going on in it. They would tirelessly preach God's love to me. I would not hear it, though.

The world and all that it offered became more and more appealing to me the further I slipped away from God. My decision to choose the party scene over the God scene left a door open wide for Satan to casually stroll into my life and hand me every lie he could conjure. I began to believe that I wasn't worthy of the life that God desired for me. I slowly accepted the falsehoods that the enemy introduced as facts of life, forgetting that I was made in God's image and that God loved me unconditionally. Things began to spiral out of control. Buying all that Satan had to sell, I plunged headfirst into darkness, believing that I would create my own happiness somehow or at least find a way to escape my misery. At that point, the party life began to develop a luster that was bright enough to blind me of reason, and drugs sang out empty promises that I was sure they would keep.

I had been drinking and smoking pot for a while, but I was about to enter into a world I never knew existed, and that world was built on cocaine. My first line of cocaine sent me over the top! I had never felt pretty before, and when I took that hit, I felt on top of the world. Here is what I had sought for so long: confidence in the form of white powder. There was a downfall, of course, in that as soon as the high faded, so did my reestablished sense of self-worth, so another hit had to be taken, and the cycle of destruction began.

I was seventeen when I got hooked on cocaine; all it took was one hit to reel me in, and I was a slave to that powdery white substance. I had found the Novocain for the root canal that was my life. The stockpile of hurts and insecurities born from my past slowly died away with every line. I was vulnerable to anything that would cover up all my insincerity; I wanted to feel good about me, and I didn't care what path I had to take to do that. I had to hide the real me, the hurting me, and now I had found a way. Unfortunately, cocaine was just like makeup on a burn victim. It covered the scars, but they still loomed beneath the façade and so did the pain from their source.

Later in 2002 I began waiting tables at one of the restaurants in Tyler, Texas, and my partying continued. I started to fall in with a group of fellow partiers that began to feel like real friends. I was a very outgoing person, so almost everyone I met liked to be around me. I was the life of the party. I had constructed a fantastic mask that I wore at all times to hide the pain and hurt I carried with me. A smile was plastered to my face, but inside I was dying. I just wanted to be accepted by people. Whatever I had to do to win them over, I would, even if that meant selling my soul to the devil himself. I surrounded myself with faux friends, parties, drugs, alcohol, and men. My life was a circus, but I was the ringleader now. All eyes were on me.

I went through so much looking for someone to love me. All I wanted from life was to feel real, unconditional love, but all my life I had felt shoved aside. From the time I was a little girl, I had decided that I was unlovable. As a child, it seemed to me that my sisters, especially my little sister, were stealing what was mine, my father's affection. I fought for my father's attention but felt I was always in a losing battle. As I grew older, I realized that my father wasn't the only man whom I could get attention from, and I pursued those other men at every opportunity. Most of the time those pursuits were disastrous, but on one occasion, the guy I was after actually proved to be worth it.

I remember walking into work one sunny afternoon. As I made my way to the kitchen, I noticed the guy standing behind the bar. This guy I wanted to get to know better. It was one of those moments that actually does take your breath away. I became a little flushed on first seeing him, but I regained composure, started to breathe again, and glanced at his name tag, Jonathan. He was around six feet tall with these beautiful green eyes and jet-black hair. He was gorgeous.

Jonathan had been transferred from another store and was our new bartender. He was very quiet and shy, which was a little different for me because I was loud and outgoing. He was a challenge, though, and I wasn't about to lose. I was on a mission, and his name was Jonathan. After a while, he loosened up and became one of us. We started hanging out and spending a lot of time together. He was a genuinely good guy. He would cuddle me, and we would fall asleep. I was looking for more than cuddling, though. He never made advances, however, and I was afraid it would ruin a good thing anyway. I knew it was because he respected me, and I didn't want anything to ruin our friendship, so we remained just friends. He was one of a kind. I had never met anyone quite like him. There was just something about him that captured me and would not let me go.

Jonathan had become one of my closest friends, and I knew that I could rely on him. He was there for me to celebrate when I was happy and support me when I was down. That new bartender was absolutely everything that I had been looking for. He was kind and gentle yet strong, the perfect man in so many ways. Before I knew it, I was sincerely and completely in love with this guy. I was so afraid to tell him that I loved him, though. I was terrified that he would reject me; that would kill me. I had become calloused while I was on the road with my family, and I wasn't about to break the thick skin I had developed now. I didn't tell him at that time how I really felt, not because I didn't want to but because I was afraid. Fear and insecurity stepped in my way like it always did.

Although I never told Jonathan exactly what he meant to me, we shared something special, even if it wasn't as much as I would like it to be. He was there for me in my rough times, and I was there for him in his. One night we were lying on his bed talking and laughing; I looked up at him and said, "Jonathan, one day I am going to marry you." He just smiled. I believed he was my soul mate, and nothing he would do was going to change that. There were nights we would crawl up on the rooftop of his house and stare at the stars. He was the only thing in the world that made me feel as good as the drugs did, but there was no comedown or hangover with him. Those were the days, but like everything else I had known in life, I knew that those times would probably have to fade away.

———— ◆ ————

One winter night in 2003, my girlfriend, Alice, set me up on a blind date with her gorgeous cowboy friend,

Jacob. We meet up in the Walmart parking lot in town. When he stepped out of his white 4x4 diesel truck, I thought, *Hmm, he's a stud.* His jeans and shirt were starched, and this man was well put together. He had dark-brown hair with bright green eyes and stood about five feet eight inches—a little short for me, but he was handsome. He introduced himself and then opened the door for me to jump in. I got up in the truck, and we headed off for our night on the town.

Jacob was a gentleman and said all the right things. By the time the evening was over, I was ready for our next date. It was a fast fall with this guy. He was a charmer and swept me right into his spider web.

I had been warned that he used to sell dope and was addicted to meth at one time, but none of that mattered to me because of how he made me feel. He had also just gotten out of prison after serving some time in safe pee, which was a kind of rehabilitation/jail. I didn't care what his past was, though. He was good looking, and he was interested in me.

As we spent more time together, Jacob and I got to talking about our lives, and he gave me a short story of his life before prison. He told me that he was a big dealer and manufacturer of meth and was hooked on it himself at one time, which eventually led him to prison. He claimed that he was clean and sober now, though, and that he wanted a better life for himself. If he was to do it again, however, it would be with the needle; he didn't like it any other way. That is what one calls a "red flag."

When I asked Jacob how it felt to do dope that way, he said it was the best way to do it, but once you start it, you wouldn't want it any other way. I personally had never really liked meth much, and I had never used a needle. My drug of choice was still cocaine. I was willing to try anything once, though, so I had to try it. I had to know how it felt to shoot dope through my veins.

When I was introduced to the needle, my life rapidly changed. I knew what it was like to smoke crack cocaine and to snort powder cocaine, but how would it feel to shoot into my vein? I had seen enough movies with people shooting up to get an idea by their expressions afterward. They looked euphoric. They seemed not to have a care in the world; nothing mattered. Before the needle even touched my skin, I knew I would eventually be one of them.

Before long, Alice, Jacob, and I were always together. We were a modern-day version of *Three's Company*, and drug use was our shared apartment, the glue that kept us together. They were recovering addicts, and I was on the road to becoming one. They both had experienced drugs the same way, with the needle, and agreed for them it was the only way to truly get high. The more they raved about the power of the almighty needle, the more curious I became. You know what they say, "Curiosity killed the cat."

One February night, I decided I was going to find out what was so amazing about the needle. I said to myself, *One time isn't going to hurt me*. Resolute to no longer have virgin veins, I made a call that would change my life forever. Alice, Jacob, and I drove to pick up the dope. I was about to have an experience that would blow away any experience I'd had up to that point, an experience that would resonate in the core of my being and lead me down roads I never imagined.

They warned me that once I used a needle, I would never go back. They were right. We got to Alice's house, and she mixed up the water and cocaine in a spoon, then took the needle and drew up thirty units of dope into the syringe. After that, she tied off her arm and pierced her skin, probing for a vein. This wasn't her first time. She hit the vein and pushed the stopper, pumping a teaspoon of reality-be-gone into her body. Once the needle was removed, she leaned her head back and let herself feel every detail of the high. A few minutes passed, and it was my turn. She did the same thing as before, but with my arm and my vein. She pulled up half the amount she did for herself into the syringe. Because this was my first time, she didn't want to give me too much.

Alice flicked the needle and looked up at me. "Are you ready?"

I stared down at the needle and then up at Alice and nodded.

"Hold your arm tightly with your right hand, and pump your fist with your left so I can see your vein clearly." Alice gave me orders the same way a nurse might when having blood drawn at the doctor's office.

I did just what she said and my vein popped right up. At that moment, she stabbed my arm with the needle, and the drug burst through my vein. I was speechless.

This was absolutely nothing I had ever felt. It was like the second that needle entered my vein that my DNA reshaped itself. Sensations were different, color was different, and the air I breathed was different. They were right; once you cross over, there is no coming back.

From that moment forward, I was wrapped up in Satan's web of deceit. Drugs were the most amazing lie he had ever told me, and I was willing to believe it all as long as this high didn't go away. Being high, especially needle high, was an escape from myself, my body, and everything in life I didn't want to deal with. I was now on my way to being a full-blown needle junky.

As my relationships with needles got more serious, so did my relationship with the guy who introduced me to shooting. Jacob and I become more involved with one another, and our relationship was filled with sex, alcohol, and drugs. I became wilder than before and more dependent on him to give me my next fix. I didn't know at the time how to find the vein and hit it myself, so I had to depend on him or Alice to do it for me. After a while, I was determined to do it myself and not rely on them anymore. If I had to poke myself until I was black and blue, I was going to find out how to do this. I was tired of waiting on them to get high first and then leaving me out to dry, so I said, "To hell with it. I will do it myself." I did. I learned how to hit myself with my own needle. I didn't need them anymore to get high. I wasn't on my way anymore. I *was* a full-blown junky.

All I could think about now was my next fix. I could feel the needle piercing my skin, allowing the poison to run through my vein, hitting every part of my body. Every time the needle pricked my vein, a heat came over my body that started from my toes and traveled through my legs, up to my arms, and out of the top of my head. My addiction morphed from a want to a need. I was chemically dependent on something that could take my life at any time, but I couldn't walk away; my body craved it.

I had become consumed with the feeling getting high gave me; it was a feeling of lust, beauty, and power. I had a new kind of confidence that I'd never felt, and nothing could come close to that feeling. I felt sexy for the first time. The confidence was fleeting, though, and only lasted as long as the high did. I wanted to stay high as much as possible so I wouldn't have to feel low ever again. In those moments, all my insecurities were gone, but they never failed to boomerang back. Getting high became a way of life at that point. Jacob, needles, and junk were my world.

Jacob and I ended up dating for about three months, a very tumultuous three months. We were now both meth addicts and needle junkies. Our relationship got progressively worse and was bound to end disastrously. During our relationship, I lost my job at as a server because of my drug use. I was slipping deep into this new lifestyle, and it was becoming obvious that I had a serious problem to anyone who knew me well.

Even Jonathan noticed that I was getting in over my head. I ran back to him every time I felt that I had no one to go to because I knew I could always count on him; he was my rock through all the insanity. Although he could tell that I had gotten deep into the lifestyle, he stayed by my side and did what he could to lift me up. He was worried about me, though, and he wanted me to get better. He always knew who I really was and what I was truly capable of. At that time, though, he could see my light was fading.

Jonathan was not the only person who had noticed that I was changing. Many people could see a transformation in me within those couple of months after I had become so well acquainted with the needle; everyone but I could see it. I honestly didn't want to face that I had became a junky, but there was no way around it; a junky was exactly what I was. I maintained a nice cover up by being a high-maintenance junky with nice clothes, my makeup done perfectly, and hair always in place, but I never went anywhere without a needle.

I didn't care if I lost everything. The only thing that mattered was my next fix. In an attempt to gain some control over my life and my insecurities, I had lost any bit of control I had. I was now a hopeless addict, and there was nothing that anyone could do to change that.

Jacob eventually told me that he couldn't do this anymore; if he didn't stop and put down the needle, it was going to cost him his freedom again. He stopped the drugs for a while, but I knew I couldn't. I craved it too badly. I needed the drugs. They were the cure for all that ailed me. I actually liked myself for once, but I knew it wouldn't last if I didn't keep the needle in my arm. I couldn't let reality catch up with me, so I kept on using until I was so far gone that even Jacob, the person who got me into all of this, didn't want anything to do with me anymore.

Jacob ultimately left me. I was completely devastated. The memories of the conversation we had are burned in my mind. When I heard him say on the other end of the phone that he didn't want to be with me anymore, a piece of me withered and died. I was broken again. It was the feeling I had when I was a little girl and my parents were divorcing; someone who was supposed to love me had betrayed me. He wasted no time detoxing from me, either. He completely vanished; just like that, he was gone. Jacob left me hollower than I'd ever been. There is not much worse than a heartbroken junky.

Once again, I ran to the one person who might be able to console me. I took what was left of the broken me to Jonathan who, like always, did all he could to put me back together. He wanted so badly to fix me, and I desperately wanted to be fixed, but Jacob had made a deep wound that wasn't going to easily heal. The sting of rejection and the burdening weight of hopelessness seemed unbearable at times. What Jacob's leaving left in its wake was an even harder junky with a shattered heart. My parents tried to console me, but they didn't know what to do. They would get as close to me as I would allow, which wasn't very, and pray the rest of the time. I would disappear into my room for days and not eat or sleep. What my parents didn't realize is that while I was hiding away in my bedroom isolating myself from everyone, I was also getting high to deal with my hurt.

I regretted ever meeting Jacob. He had caused me nothing but grief, more grief than I thought possible for one person to cause another. He introduced me to needles, dragged me along while he got the last bit of partying out of his system, and then abandoned me when he was ready to get off the merry-go-round of addiction. I was only a phase for him, but he was something I had come to depend on. I didn't know where to turn at this point. I had chosen Jacob and needles over Jonathan, only to have Jacob leave like everyone else in my past had. I felt like I had no one. I was officially hitting rock bottom.

One Sunday afternoon I went for a drive to clear my head. As I drove around town listening to a song by Brooks and Dunn, "The Long Good-bye," I decided that I could not handle any of this anymore; that I couldn't take Jacob leaving or the fact that I needed a needle in my arm to feel normal. I stopped by a pharmacy, picked up a bottle of sleeping pills, and headed back home.

When I pulled up in the driveway, I got out of my red Dodge Stratus with the bottle of sleeping pills in my purse. I walked up the ramp to our house, through the back door, and down the hall of the sunroom into my bedroom. I didn't say a word to anyone in the house. I had decided that I wasn't going to live like this anymore, and I was determined to do what it took to stop.

I knew that the feelings I had were not going to go quietly and right at that moment they were screaming. Regret, fear, disgust, and spite swelled inside me. I had been cheated in so many ways, and, as far as I could see with my resentful teenage eyes, nothing was going to change for me; life would always be there to make sure I was dealt a bad hand.

I would rather die a thousand deaths than to be a junky and alone. In my hand was a bottle of over-the-counter sleeping pills, its two-tone blue label hidden behind my clenched, white knuckles. I pried the top from the bottle and dumped every pill into my mouth, swallowing them all in one determined gulp with a glass of water by my bed. With the pills swallowed, I lay down and relaxed, waiting for the drowsiness to overtake me.

Right about the time I should've felt the relief of knowing it was all almost over, my mind began to race. Everything about my life to this point danced through my mind: my childhood, my family, the people I had met, God. Was I really ready to die? I just wanted to feel normal. I longed to know what real happiness felt like. I wanted a life with less pain. I was so out of control, though. The drugs had consumed me. The answer I was looking for was God, of course, but I wasn't ready to receive Him. Although I knew then that I wasn't ready for God, I started to question if I was ready for death.

After about a half hour, my eyes became heavy, and I felt as if I were detaching from everything around me. I knew the pills were taking effect and that my life was coming to an end. At that moment, I realized I didn't want to die; I just wanted the pain to stop. I got up and went into my parents' room.

"I'm sorry." The words floated in the air and sounded strange.

"Honey, what is it?" my mom asked, looking up at me from where she sat. It was obvious that something was wrong.

"I'm just so tired of everything right now. I can't do it anymore, so I took a bottle of sleeping pills." I had mixed emotions as I started to confess what I had just done.

"How many did you take?" my dad asked with panic building in his voice.

"I don't know, a bottle. I just took the entire bottle. I don't want to hurt anyone. I just can't do this anymore." I was sincere but detached as I spoke.

My parents called 911. When the ambulance arrived, I was still conscious, but I was on my way out. I was rushed to the emergency room for observation. When I arrived, they placed me in a small room off to the side where I received treatment for the suicide attempt. Nurses came in and pumped my stomach, sticking a tube down my throat with black charcoal to pull the poison out of my body. The feeling was terrible.

Lying in that hospital bed, I came to my senses and realized that it was crazy to kill myself over a failed relationship, especially one that was so destructive. I just wanted the pain to stop, not to die. There is just something about pain that is unbearable for me; it torments me and pushes me to react in harsh ways. I didn't care what I had to do to be rid of it that day. I just wanted to stop hurting and live again. Ironically, I handled it by trying to end my life. I saw no other escape. The pains of losing something you love, even if it's harmful, can destroy you if you let it.

The addiction I had to Jacob was as destructive as anything else I had become addicted to. It almost destroyed my life. Not only did our relationship introduce me to needles, the end of it pushed me into full-on bulimia. Where purging had been an infrequent thing in my past, after my breakup with Jacob, I had dedicated myself fully to the disease. It destroyed me in other ways too, though. I was already dead before I took those pills—emotionally dead. What I did that day was a cry for help. I didn't want to die; I wanted someone to see that I was dying.

The hospital released me within hours. When I returned home, I thought, *Where do I go from here?* I had to start over and let the past be the past, but that was a little hard for me. I don't let things go easily. I tend to cling to things longer than I probably should sometimes. I guess that was a problem created from my past. The six years we traveled the country, all I did was love and leave; letting go and leaving was part of my daily routine it seemed. My fear was that people would always walk out on me, so that made me cling to them even more. I was an emotional leech, sucking the life right out of anyone I wanted to be close to.

To remedy my problem and be sure I would never be hurt again, I built up an impenetrable wall around my heart at that point. I was determined that no one would ever hurt me again. The problem with building up walls that can't be broken down is that they don't allow anything in. In an attempt to save myself from future hurt, I created an emotional barrier that no one could penetrate, regardless of their intentions.

Within months after my suicide attempt, instead of wiping the slate clean, I allowed more bitterness to set in, and my heart became harder. No one would ever break me again. I had adopted the attitude that I would destroy someone before they could touch me. My goal was to offer people the same treatment I had received. I would use deceit and lies to get what I needed and then toss people away when I had gotten what I wanted. No one stood a chance with me.

My heart was full of malevolence and hate—hate for God and His creation. My soul was a void. God was nothing to me. In my mind, He had let me down. I felt all alone and uncertain about my future and what would become of me. My life was tiny segments of broken dreams and bad experiences.

I had to move past everything up to this point if I was going to make it, and I knew it, but where could I start? Things had gotten so complicated. There was so much that I carried with me that I couldn't just will away. I knew that dying wasn't the answer. I had gone down that path, but I also didn't know how I was supposed to live. Moving on with your life sounds so easy. People will say, "Just pick up and move on." We are a collection of memories and experiences from our past, though. What do we have left if we just leave everything behind? Even the things that cause pain help build what we are. Letting go of those things felt a little like disappearing.

CHAPTER FIVE

INSANITY

During the time I spent trying to figure out what to do after my suicide attempt, I met my future best friend, Elizabeth Layne. She was relentless in her support for me, there for me through absolutely everything, good and bad. Elizabeth was a good girl. When we first met, she didn't do much partying, so we were different in that aspect, but that didn't matter to either of us.

Elizabeth and I had a friendship that was one of a kind; we were connected at the heart. She was the definition of a true friend. She knew about all the demons I struggled with but loved me anyway. I became very close to her and her family. I was just another one of their girls. Her parents didn't know about my drug addiction, though. I had mastered the art of hiding it. I was what you would call a functioning addict; I would be high and still function in life. I had learned how to manipulate and deceive people that well.

Soon, Elizabeth got her own place, and the party really started. She wouldn't be a good girl for much longer. She was twenty, I was nineteen, and life was ours. We spent countless nights getting high, staying out all night hitting the clubs, and going wherever the wind would take us. We were both outgoing with lots of friends. We loved being with people. Most of our nights we were hanging out with our friends, playing cards or dominoes, and snorting cocaine or whatever was there.

Elizabeth knew that I was on the needle, and one night she asked me to let her try it. I was hesitant at first, but then agreed. I regret the day I put the needle into her arm. I did the very thing I said I would never do. I promised myself after all that happened with Jacob that I would never do to someone else what was done to me, but that night, I did just that.

It took no time at all for Elizabeth and me to get in over our heads. We were both strung out on dope, and the friendship that meant so much to me ended in disaster. Her family found out about our drug use and put a stop to our friendship. I was distraught. Our relationship was more than just drugs and parties; it was heartfelt. I had lots of friends, but she was the only real friend whom I could count on except for Jonathan. When she wasn't around anymore, I blamed myself, and I ran straight to Jonathan for comfort. I had lost one of my best friends, and I needed him to tell me that I would be okay. Jonathan was there for me like he always was, and it meant the world to me that he was, but it still couldn't undo what had been done. I had lost someone very special to me, and even though

Jonathan's support meant a lot, I wanted that special someone back.

If I hadn't introduced her to the life of chaos, maybe we would have made it. What I couldn't see then, though, was that God was protecting her from what was about to come. If she would have been with me any longer, she may have traveled the same path I was about to. Regardless of the reasoning, however, feeling that my one true friend was gone, I took a deeper dive to the bottom.

———◆·◆———

Losing my best friend to my drug addiction did not lead me out of the lifestyle I had fallen into. In fact, it made the whole situation worse. I had reached a point that few come back from. Only God could have saved me, but I had set up a barrier that wouldn't allow God in. I was absolutely miserable, which meant that I now had to use nonstop to escape my reality.

At that point, my drug use was no secret to anyone. I was in and out of my parents' house. I would disappear and stay high and then come back to try to detox. I would make it for one or two days, but it never failed. I would ultimately leave to go out and find some more dope and disappear for a while. I just could not do it; I couldn't walk away from drugs. I physically hurt when I tried.

When I would stay away from my parents' house, I didn't do it to hurt them; I did it to survive and to save them. I wasn't getting high just for the feeling anymore; I was doing it because I would get sick if I didn't. I had reached a point that I had to use, and I didn't want my parents to have to watch me as I destroyed myself. I would make this coming and going a regular thing from that point on, but I always did it for them, or at least that was my intention. Sure, I was angry, but I still loved them, and I didn't want to hurt them.

The times I would come back home in an attempt to clean up, my parents would do what they could to pull me back in and get me to let God work in my life. My dad would always give me Christian CDs to listen to, and my mom would sit with me up in my room, and we would listen to one particular song, "In Your Presence," on repeat. The songs from the CDs and the lyrics from "In Your Presence" would sneak in my mind at the strangest times. I would be doped up and almost unconscious, but I would hear those songs in my head.

Every time I left my parents' house to find another fix, they would beg me not to go. They would ask that I just stay and give up the drugs that were causing so much hurt and destruction. They would remind me that I was lying on the kitchen floor wailing the day before because of them and ask that I just let them go now and let God take their place. I couldn't though. I needed them. Regardless of the pleas, I would pack up and leave. They would stand in the front yard with tears streaming down their face while I headed down the street toward the closest dealer's house.

＊

My rejection of God had been somewhat implicit the entire time I was in and out of my parents' home. In spring of 2004, however, I made my grievance with God official. If God or my family had any questions about my feelings, they would no longer have to wonder.

One evening at church during a sermon, I sat at the back of my dad's church while God moved at the front. There was a guest speaker that night, and God was definitely present. Even someone as lost as me could tell that. As I sat in the very back pew, uninterested in what was going on at the front of the church, God made his way back to me and spoke to me, and He asked me to give up the life I had created and follow Him. I said no.

After all I had been through, what reason did I have to follow God and live my life for Him? I could not think of one instance that God had ever helped me out, so I wasn't about to build my life around Him. With a tear-streaked face, I let God know right then that I was not interested in His offer. I got up to leave the church after I turned my back on God. As I was leaving, the guest speaker somehow saw me at the back of the church rushing for the door.

"Who is that?" the evangelist leaned over and asked my dad.

"That's my daughter," my dad responded, staring back at me and shaking his head.

"She's running from God," the evangelist replied, keeping his eyes fixed on me.

Suddenly, the evangelist quit talking to my dad and spoke clearly into the microphone and directly at me, "You can run from God, but He will always find you."

We'll see, I thought as I exited the church. I was just like Jonah that day, running from God after He had called me specifically. I would hit my storm and be thrown into the turbulent sea just like Jonah soon enough, too.

I never went back to church after that day. I didn't see that there was any reason to. I was angry, really angry, that God had let so much happen to me, and I felt betrayed. The day that so many people walked out on my family in Valliant, Oklahoma, I developed a wounded spirit. I was deeply scarred by what the church had done to my family, and that hurt grew with every person who let me down or let me go thereafter, and I was taking it out on God. I had found a new god, anyway, in cocaine, so I would be fine. I was going to have to use a lot more now, though. It takes a lot of cocaine to fill a God-sized hole. I was bound to do it though, which meant I had to use constantly.

One of the many problems with using nonstop is that the habit gets to be pretty pricey. The snowball effect of addiction is also that keeping a job is impossible. I managed to keep a job at a department store as a makeup consultant for almost an entire year, and I did really well there, too, but my drug use and ability to work had an indirect correlation to one another.

The first six months or so working at the department store, no one I worked would've ever guessed that I was a user. As time passed, however, and the weight dropped away, people began to notice. I had become close with some of the women I worked with, and they became seriously concerned with my health. They even called my parents at one point.

After a little less than a year, I was finally fired from the department store. I had become unreliable and didn't really care anymore if I had a job or not anyway. I had met an older man named Jeff a couple years before whom I knew would take care of me if all else failed, so I wasn't terribly worried about my makeup job. I did try a couple of times after the department store, but nothing stuck. I already had a full-time job anyway, and it was called the needle, and it came second to none.

I would keep it together long enough to make it through an interview and maybe get through the training process. After that, it didn't take anyone I worked for long to realize that I was not going to be employee of the month anytime soon. One by one, I lost every job I got. Without a job, I didn't have any disposable income. Without disposable income, there was no way for me to support my growing habit. I didn't have many options at this point. I could either attempt a life of sobriety or find a different alternative to make sure I would not have to worry about where my next fix would come from. Sobriety was out of the question, so Jeff it would be. He seemed to be the answer to all my problems—all my problems concerning money and drugs, anyway.

I was around eighteen when I first met Jeff, so I had actually known him for a few years by the time I lost my job and couldn't stick to a new one. He was an older man, much older. Jeff was a blessing and a curse, there to save me from any trouble I would get into, but also there to provide all the things I needed to get into trouble. The biggest problem that Jeff created in my life was that he acted as a false sense of security for me. Things never seemed as bad as they really were, so I was never able to see the gravity of the situation.

When our relationship started, it seemed innocent enough. He was an older guy who wanted to feel young again, and I was a young woman shackled with drug addiction and abandonment issues. We were a match made in heaven. I would go out with Jeff, and everyone would see him with a pretty young girl on his arm, and he would make sure I had enough money to live the life I wanted to live at that time. That was one of Jeff's biggest perks; he had plenty of money to spend, and he didn't mind spending it on me.

Because of Jeff, I was able to be a full-blown junky but fly under the junky radar. If you saw me walk in a room, you would never guess that just before I got out of my car I had shoved a needle in my arm. I could ignore what I was becoming because I didn't fit the description of a hardcore addict. Speed addicts were living on the streets, begging for change on corners for their next fix, and wearing duct taped shoes. I was driving a luxury car and wearing fur. Junkies did not wear fur.

One thing that I failed to notice while I was on shopping sprees and receiving flowers on a weekly basis was this guy, Jeff, was going to be the death of me. Although Jeff had nothing but good intentions, as odd as that sounds, at the end of the day, what he was to me was a sugar daddy, and sugar daddies are generally in the business of using a girls' insecurities to get what they need, not to offer them help to restore what was broken inside them. Jeff saw that I was completely lost, and he used that. It wasn't that he didn't care about me in his own sordid way, but part of that perverse love was that he needed me to be strung out. An attractive, sober twenty-one-year-old woman doesn't generally spend all of her free time with a man in his fifties. Jeff was not oblivious to this fact, so he made sure that I didn't have to go far to find my next fix.

Although Jeff did find it advantageous to have me addicted, he did do some things that I can say could have saved my life. When I got myself into sticky situations, Jeff would always come to my rescue. I could call him at any time of the night anywhere, and, if I was in trouble, Jeff would come to the rescue. That is what was so dangerous about him; he saved me so often that I couldn't see that he was ruining me. See, I had Jonathan throughout this that I knew I could count on, but he didn't support the habit for me the way Jeff did, so I made the poor choice of an addict, and I clung to the sordid relationship that Jeff provided instead of leaning completely on the true and genuine friendship that Jonathan was always there to offer me.

Jeff wasn't a bomb in a pretty package only because of his ability to save me when I should have been left to sink; he was also furtively destructive because he hid the severity of my problem from me. He kept me from being an outward manifestation of what I truly was. Soon, though, I would get so caught up in the drug game that even Jeff's furs wouldn't cover my problems up.

When I first started using, selling drugs never crossed my mind. I couldn't have imagined there would ever be a reason to do such a thing. It was strange, though, how naturally I fell into it. There is this process that addicts seem to go through that slowly prepares them for lifestyles that your everyday person could never imagine. A normal person rarely just wakes up one morning and decides to go into the narcotic distribution business. It is something that takes some time and a hardcore dedication to drugs to work up to. I had both of those, though, and had graduated from the school of the hardcore junky. I was about to make my debut into the business side of drugs. I had always been an overachiever when it came to addictive substances, so it was only natural that I would begin to sell.

When I began to sell dope, I was exposed to many of the horrors that addiction has to offer. First of all, because I was now on the inside of the drug operation, I actually knew some people who cooked. The making of illegal drugs turns your everyday junky into an unlicensed chemist, and it doesn't take a wild imagination or a lot of insight to realize that anyone who goes days without eating or sleeping and is prone to drug-induced hallucinations does not need to be mixing explosive chemicals together. Addiction can be blinding, though, so I would actually go into labs as people I knew cooked.

From time to time, I would have flashes of how ridiculous I had become. I would suddenly realize how wrapped up I had gotten and wonder how I'd reached this point. I would think about how many first timers I would get to, how many junkies like me it would offer a quick fix to, and even how many people might take their last bang from me because of finally deciding it was enough, getting caught, or because they had pulled a little too much this time and their heart couldn't handle the dosage. My skin would start to ache from want, though, and those thoughts would dissipate as my craving took over. This is just what I was now. Like everything else in life, using helped me ignore what my selling was actually doing. What a perfect little setup; I had the problem and the solution right in the same cellophane bag.

I started out fairly small, selling Methamphetamines, meth, to people in the area. As time went by, though, things started to escalate. To anyone who doesn't have experience with addiction or selling, you don't generally stand in place as either a user or a seller; you have to move up or more out in most cases. This means that you tend to sell bigger, use more, and lose more of your soul. Drugs had become the center that my life revolved around. Almost every part of my life tied back to them somehow; I used them to fill voids alongside my eating disorder, used them to make friends, and used them to use them.

I had spent a lot of my life draped in insecurity. I had struggled with my weight and a fear of rejection. When I started selling, though, I found my niche. I was finally the best at something, and everyone I knew thought I was amazing. Although I harbored a lot of self-doubt deep down, the surface me, especially the high surface me, was the most charismatic person you could meet.

When dealing on my own wasn't enough for me, I became involved with a drug cartel. This meant that I was no longer just a local dealer. I had made it to the big time. Being involved with a drug cartel meant a lot. First of all, it meant that I belonged to something, that I wasn't alone. As strange as this may sound, that was a comfort to me. That, my friends, is addiction. I felt comforted by being involved with people who, if they got paranoid about my involvement with the police or if I decided that I didn't want to be involved with drug running anymore, could very well hurt, or even kill, me or my loved ones. It was something to cling to, though, so I did. The cartel gave me a false sense of belonging, and I would take any sense of belonging I could find.

The second thing that being involved with a drug cartel meant was that the false, dysfunctional family of drug manufacturers, dealers, and runners replaced my real family. I could no longer play the role of Janie the middle daughter and sister along with Janie the drug runner, so I had to choose one. Like always, my addiction won the toss-up, so I became completely cut off from my family. They wouldn't hear from me for months at a time. While I was out dealing and running, my parents were home praying and keeping in constant contact with God, asking Him to keep me safe.

Even Jonathan, who had loved me so sincerely, was beginning to drift away because of my problem. At that point, we really began to fall apart. Seeing me bounce from place to place, getting worse by the day and unable to even keep a job anymore, Jonathan decided that he could not sit by and watch me kill myself anymore. He told me that I needed to quit, that he couldn't go on being a part of my life if I didn't. I had to decide between Jonathan and drugs. I wanted so badly to tell him that I would walk away for him, but walking away isn't easy for an addict, and I just couldn't do it, not even for him.

Jonathan laid it all out on the table for me. He told me that he couldn't do any of this anymore with me, no matter how much he wanted to. He told me that he could no longer be there for me—that our friendship was over. With his words, Jonathan took all that was important to me. Of course, it was drugs, not Jonathan, who stole everything I loved, but in the moment, I felt the painful sting of the most intense rejection of my life and did all I could think to do; I packed up what I could and headed to Dallas to get away from everything and everyone—except for my good friend the needle, of course.

I moved to Dallas for a short time and got involved in heroine. I was still involved with the cartel, and my life continued to go downhill. My life in Dallas had gotten completely crazy, but I ended up coming back after only about six months and settling back down, if you can call it that, in Tyler.

While I was in Dallas, my parents had no idea what was going on with me; they didn't know where I was, who I was staying with, or even if I was on the streets or in jail. I had a phone, and my dad would call me every day in an attempt to get a hold of me, but I would just ignore him or answer and be short with him. I never would tell him where I was. They figured with me in Tyler, at least they had a chance of tracking me down or being there when I may need them. This was a good thing for me because one night, I needed them.

Being an experienced junky should mean that you know exactly what you can handle as far as dope goes. Unfortunately for us junkies, we are always chasing the dragon, so we tend to do just a little more than we can handle in an attempt to feel the way we did the first time we ever shot up. I was no exception to the rule. One night, I almost caught the dragon, and that is not a good thing.

It's hard to remember the details, but I know that I pulled too much, and one of my best friends and roommates, Rick, had gotten a hold of my parents once I started to overdose. They picked me up from the hotel room I was in and rushed me to the emergency room. After treating me, the doctor had some advice for my dad.

"Your daughter in there is messed up in dope in a bad way, Mr. Burkett," the doctor said, his arms crossed over his chest.

"I know that," my dad said, looking past the doctor as he spoke, "but I have no idea what we're supposed to do."

"Let her crash," the doctor said in one quick breath.

"Let her crash?" my dad asked, agitated that he was standing there receiving parenting advice from a physician who probably had no children of his own.

"That's right. You need to let her fall hard if you want her to get out of this alive. She's got to be scared straight. That means that mom and dad have to step back and let her hit rock bottom," the doctor said, staring straight into my dad's eyes.

"Let me ask you something." My dad was getting close to angry now. "What would you do if that were your little girl in there? Would you just abandon her?"

"Probably not, but that doesn't mean that it would be the right thing to do." The doctor's tone started to shift from matter-of-fact to empathetic. "I see it all the time, though. It will be tough, but it has to be done."

My dad thanked the doctor for his suggestion and then walked away. That doctor may have seen it all the time, but my dad didn't care. He knew I needed him and my mom, and he was not going to give up on me, even if I had given up on myself. Now that I was closer to home, he would be sure that he took care of me. He would not stand by and let me crash as long as he could get to me.

Even though I was no longer hours away, it wasn't easy for my parents to keep tabs on me. I had no permanent home and jumped from hotel to hotel with my two best friends, Rick (who called my parents when I overdosed) and Chris. My life was complete chaos, and it revolved around drugs. With drugs as the focal point of my existence, my life was erratic and dangerous to say the least. I was paranoid every second of the day and didn't leave the hotel without a switchblade. My home address changed weekly, as my cohorts and I moved constantly from one place to the next to try to stay one step ahead of the cops. When I was a kid, I would've given anything to stay in one place; now, I wouldn't allow myself to be still.

Although they were lost in the world with me, Rick and Chris were also guardian angels while I was bouncing from suites and motel rooms, keeping a needle in my arm at all times. Rick would call my parents to let them know that I was okay or when I needed help, and Chris would make sure that I was safe, or as safe as a dealer can be. They became my family, and I trusted in them. I did nothing without them—until our lifestyle finally caught up with us, that is.

One night, my dad found me in a hotel room, blown out of my mind. When I answered the door, I could tell that whatever he had to say was urgent. The second I answered the door, he began to speak.

"I need you to come with me, Janie." It was a statement, not a question.

"What?" I was lit and had no idea what was going on.

"I need you to get in the car with me and come with me. We have to talk."

Although I usually made it a point to resist any kind of help or good advice at the juncture in my life, there was something about my dad's tone and the expression on his face that urged me to go with him. Not to ask any questions, just to go. That is what I did. We both got into my dad's car, and he started driving.

"Listen to me, Janie, you cannot start selling drugs."

This was insane. For a second, I thought it was the dope. I hadn't slept in a couple of days. This was a hallucination, a projection of my subconscious or something. It had to be. I couldn't fathom what would make my dad come to me and say this right now or how he had any idea about my involvement with selling.

"The Holy Spirit talked to me, Janie, and told me that you cannot sell or you will go to jail. This is serious, sweetheart. You have to listen to me."

I had no idea what to make of all this. My dad's intensity definitely shook me, but I wasn't sure that I was ready to heed warnings from anyone just yet. I made an empty promise to appease my dad, got out of the car, and went right back to doing what I was doing. When I walked out on God, I walked out on taking His help too. I didn't think I needed God anymore, so what was I going to do with warning from the Holy Spirit? I was going to brush it off and keep my back to God, even if He was reaching out to me.

While I was giving God the cold shoulder, my family was praying night and day for my well-being. They had people across the country praying for me. Because God is a loving God, He saved me from death, even though I rejected Him daily.

> For it is by grace you have been saved, through faith—and this not from yourselves, it is the gift of God.
>
> Ephesians 2:8 (NIV)

In the depths of my addiction, I was reaching a point that soon God would not even be able to save me from, however. There are few places that are out of God's reach, but I was about to hit the pits of hell, and it was going to take something drastic to change that. My mother began to pray for something different. Knowing that I was so far gone that I would likely not return to her in anything other than a body bag or a police car, she began to pray that I would be arrested. Irony doesn't begin to touch it. I was so lost that my mom was asking God to have me incarcerated to save me from myself and from those around me. It didn't take long for God to answer her prayers.

CHAPTER SIX

FINDING THE BOTTOM

In February of 2006, just shy of my twenty-second birthday, I experienced what anyone whose life is so engrossed in drugs is bound to experience: I was arrested for the very first time. This was a pivotal point for me because, up to this point, I had lived in the drug world unscathed, as far as major incidents or run-ins with the law are concerned, anyway. An early morning gas station run changed that, though.

A friend and I decided at around two in the morning that we needed to run down to a convenience store near the hotel I was staying in. We had been partying all night, as we often were, so these late-night gas station runs were nothing out of the ordinary. We walked into the store, our pupils bursting out past our irises and framed in red. It was clear that we were blown.

By this time of the night, our bodies were full of every chemical you could imagine, which made our decision-making skills less than reliable. By that time, I was a meth addict; my drug of my choice was no longer cocaine. I had started out with cocaine in the beginning, but then my addiction got harder and harder. Cocaine turned to crack cocaine, then came meth; after meth I took heroine for a test drive, and then came the pill form of heroine, and eventually I went to pills and alcohol, but right at that moment, it was meth. I loved meth more than anything. If I got too high, then I would take something to come down, mixing every kind of drug together. I smoked it out the pipe or snorted it when I didn't want to get too high, but most of the time I would just blast myself with a shot of dope, which in the addict's world we call a "bump." I had taken many a bump by the time we headed down to the gas station, the evidence of which rested in my bloodshot eyes.

The minute we passed through the gas station's advertisement-plastered glass doors, the clerk knew what was going on. She worked the graveyard shift at a gas station, so she was not unfamiliar with drunks stumbling in, trying to beat the alcohol cut off time or to buy another pack of cigarettes before they called it a night. We were much more than drunk though, and that was obvious. Before we even knew that she had spotted our bloodshot eyes, the clerk was preparing for us.

The clerk not only recognized that we were high; she also recognized me from some previous experiences, as I was kind of a regular in the place. Putting my face to my past actions, she wasted no more time in calling the cops. They were pulling in the parking lot before I could even attempt talking my way out of this. When

I saw the blue and red lights bouncing off the sliding glass doors that held the beer and soda behind the clerk, I knew that I was probably not going to walk away from this one.

My friend called Rick after I was arrested. The cops searched my car and found the dope bags and pipe. I was placed under arrest in that gas station parking lot. My charisma was not going to rescue me here. Cold, steel handcuffs were snapped into place on my wrists that looked as if they would snap under the weight, and I was put in the car. *This is it*, I thought as I sat in the back of the police car and waited for it to make its way toward the county jail.

Rick got to the gas station after I was in the cop car, hands cuffed and life over (as far as I could tell). I wasn't able to talk to Rick. I could only watch from the inside of the police car as everything took place before my eyes like a movie—or better yet, a nightmare. I could only sit and watch, mute and unable to do anything.

The officers were not impressed with Rick's chivalrous gesture in the least. As he tried to reason with them, one of the cops asked him for his ID. Rick had a warrant out for his arrest, so he was cuffed on the spot. In trying to rescue me, Rick had gotten himself arrested and would now be facing prison time. As I was being driven away in handcuffs, he was being arrested.

Not only were they taking me to jail, they were also going to search my hotel room. My dilated pupils and slurred speech gave them probable cause, along with the fact I had unknowingly sold to an undercover officer, so I was about to face some serious consequences to my life choices. We all were. I knew exactly what the police would find in that room, and none of it was going to make me look like a girl scout.

We had all been under surveillance by the DEA, so they knew that I was selling dope and what room to search. I had unknowingly been under surveillance for quite some time. For months they sat and watched, waiting to get enough information to make their case. That is where it started. I messed up there. Until that point, I had always outsmarted the cops. Or I thought I had, anyway. They were just gathering evidence, though, waiting for me to do this.

Although I was in a lot of trouble, the cop was nice and talked to me on the way to the jail. He told me that I was better than this and he bet that I even came from a good family. He was right on both accounts. He warned me to stop this nonsense and get my life on track before it got any worse, but I didn't listen.

I fought back my tears and wondered how I was going to get out of this. It was only a short drive now to graduate from dealer to criminal. It may seem odd that someone who made a living getting people hooked on drugs cared about their permanent record, but I was a little panicked as I realized I had just done something that would haunt me for the rest of my life. I could never change this, never erase it or pretend it hadn't happened. There would now be court documents and records that would prove to anyone who wanted to know that I was a criminal. My nice clothes and sports cars would not even cover this up.

When we arrived at the jail and the police officer began to lead me away from the car to the building, I was hit with an unsettling realization that roused the panic that I had felt as I was being arrested; I had no one to call. I could *not* call my dad after the promise I had made to him only days before, and all of my "friends" wouldn't step foot in a police station unless, like me, they were brought in wearing handcuffs. Jeff came to mind, though, and I suddenly wasn't too worried about getting out. I had Jeff who would quickly post my bail and get me out of this, so he was who I would call once I got the chance. Like I said before, he was always a blessing and a curse. That night, he would be a blessing.

We arrived at the jail, and I was suddenly exposed to the other side of drugs. This was not nearly as glamorous as luxury cars and minks. I was terrified. I was led into an area where they took my prints and mug shot. I stood under the yellow florescent lights, blinking back the tears as I stared straight ahead and waited for the flash to go off. My eyes were bloodshot and glassy as I stood there, from both the meth and crying. There was a heavy black outline smeared beneath my bottom lashes. I had started to look like the junky that I was.

After I was booked for possession of a control substance and possession of paraphernalia, I was taken back with the other inmates, and reality hit me so hard that I was left almost breathless. I knew that jail was no Hilton, but this I was not ready for. I began to feel a lot like livestock must when they are taken to a sale.

The first thing I had to do as an official inmate was take a shower and wash my hair with special shampoo that is intended to kill lice. It should be noted here that in jail, one no longer has the privilege of privacy. An inmate must remain in sight of an officer every step of the way. What that meant was that my shower with lice soap was done in the presence of a guard. With the lifestyle I had been leading, in and out of the strip clubs, I didn't exactly feel uncomfortable being naked in front of a stranger, but the circumstances made the experience a little dehumanizing. I know that the instances in which I had been undressed in front of people before couldn't be classified as exactly wholesome, but having someone with a gun and billy club staring at you through slit eyes felt completely different. In the other situations, I had control. Now, I was being ordered to stand there and treated as if I deserved no respect.... On second thought, maybe it wasn't so different than a lot of those other times when I stood nude in front of someone.

After showering in front of a complete stranger, the next phase of my experience was to remove my underwear. In jail, you cannot wear certain types of bras and panties. The types that they do not allow I was wearing the night I got arrested. Because I had contraband underwear, I would be given a gray jumpsuit reading "Inmate" across the back that hundreds of other inmates had worn and told to put it on without any underwear at all. I knew that jail was a place that robbed you of your freedom. What I found out early that morning was it is also a place that robs you of your dignity.

I was taken back and put in a cell with other women, hard women. I looked around me, and I saw the definition of the phrase "locked up." I was disoriented and trembling as I stood in the cell wearing a stiff gray jumpsuit and slip-on shoes, surrounded by women who were at ease in their surroundings.

As I looked around from face to face, I noticed something about the people around me. They were comfortable here; not comfortable in the way you are when you're curled up in a cozy chair with a loved one comfortable, but comfortable in the way that this wasn't anything new to them. They weren't scared about what was going to happen next or concerned about what this was going to do to their permanent record. They were pros at this. They seemed to almost take pride in the seniority they had within those cement walls. *How insane*, I thought, *to take pride in your rank at a county jail.*

Luckily this stay wasn't a long one for me. Jeff had posted my bail, and I was out within hours. I had never been so happy to be leaving a place in my life. I couldn't have stood to be around those people any longer. They were so pathetic. There were women who looked sixty and were only thirty-five, women who had no qualms about her life as a prostitute, women who bragged about what they did to get put in there. I did not belong with these people—not yet, anyway.

CHAPTER SEVEN

REVOLVING DOORS

My first experience in jail was awful. I saw what my future would be if I didn't stop in the women that surrounded me while I was there. I saw how hardened they were and how detached they seemed to be from the reality of their circumstances. They seemed almost carefree behind bars, at home and in their element. Seeing those women should've been enough to scare me straight, but it wasn't.

Just a couple of months after I had been to jail for the first time, I had another run-in with the law, but this one was kind of unique. It started with my parents going to Georgia to do a broadcast. I will explain.

In March 2006, my parents were invited to do a gospel television broadcast. This was a great opportunity for them, so they had to go. They were always leery to leave me, as I was prone to overdosing and getting arrested (when you've been arrested, it is something you don't live down, and people are constantly reminding you of it). They knew this was something that they could not pass up, though, so they explained to me that I could call them if I needed anything at all and that they would be back in no time. They assured me that I would be fine, but they were only a phone call away.

I was outraged.

God is doing it again, I thought as my parents told me they were leaving me for God's work again. I needed them right then. Couldn't they see that? They were doing what everyone else had and abandoning me. Rick and Chris were both in prison now, so my parents were all I had, and they were just going to leave me. How dare they!

I decided after shooting up one morning at 3:00 a.m. that I was going to let my parents know how I felt about their decision to just walk out on me. I scrolled down to my dad's number and listened as the phone rang on the other end.

"How dare you!" I screamed into the receiver before my dad could even ask what was wrong.

"Janie?" My dad knew that a call at this hour meant that something was wrong.

"You just up and left didn't you, Dad? That's fine by me because as far as I'm concerned, you're nothing to me!" I shouted into the phone; my words were almost incomprehensible. It must have been like listening to a two-year-old throw a temper tantrum.

"We didn't leave you, Janie. We will be home soon. I promise. What is going on?" My dad was starting to feel pretty helpless knowing that, no matter what my answer was, he was too far away to do anything.

"Oh, you don't need to come home for me. I don't need you. You stay there because I'm going to kill myself. You don't care anyway." I spit the words in violent sprays, pacing around my hotel room while I ranted.

"Janie, please stop this. You know that isn't true, and you know we love you." My dad was trying to talk me down.

"Well, I don't love you, you son of a *****! In fact, I f***** hate you!" I was past the point of no return.

"I just called to let you know that you are terrible. You both are, and I hope you burn in hell," I continued on my tirade.

My dad couldn't even respond anymore, so I kept going.

"I want to spit on the ground you walk on. You stay out of my life. You hear me? I don't want you, and I don't need you. You keep away from me." My words were sour in my mouth they were so full of hate.

"I can't stand either of you," I spit those last words and hung up the phone.

My dad got off the phone with me and called a nurse named Amy who had helped me in the hospital only days before when I had been found unconscious in my car. She happened to be a friend of a close family friend, so my dad was able to get her phone number and call her for help since they were so far away. He called her at work and explained what was going on. She immediately agreed to help.

I had no idea that my dad had called the nurse who had been so nice to me, which is good because who knows if I would even be here today if he hadn't. I was serious about not wanting his help, so I would've given her the same speech I had given him had I known he was behind what was going on. What we don't know won't hurt us, and in this case, it may have saved my life.

After talking to my dad and finding out where I was, Amy finished her shift and made her way to the motel room I was calling home at that time. She showed up at my door at 4:00 a.m. as soon as her shift was over. I just assumed she was there to check up on me since she had been so kind days before, so I let her in. I suppose a sober person may have thought a nurse showing up at four o'clock in the morning strange; luckily for both Amy and me, a person like me didn't even blink at the oddity of the whole thing.

The instant Amy saw me she knew that I had done a lot of something. She needed to call for help, so she asked me if I wanted something to eat, and I said sure. She said she'd be right back and then left the room. I sat and waited, not realizing what was happening.

When Amy returned, she had more than just burgers; she had the police with her. This did not make me happy. Again, I was taken by police, put in the back of a car, and hauled away. At the time, I was livid that this was the kind of help my parents thought I needed. I wanted someone to care about me enough to stick around, not send police to handcuff and drag me around in a cop car.

The police took me to the hospital for evaluation; then the doctors sent me to a behavioral health center where they kept me for hours. The police escorted me in handcuffs and a paper gown to the back of the van and then transferred me to the behavioral center. The doctors wanted to scare me straight by sending me there, but it didn't work. I talked my way right out of there. The doctor diagnosed me with seven different personalities but set all seven of them free.

Once I was let go, Rick's mom came and picked me up and took me back to my hotel. Rick and I were more than just friends; we were lovers, so I was pretty close to his mom, and I knew that I could trust her. When I got back to the hotel, I immediately called my dad.

"Janie?"

"Nice try, Dad." You could hear the smirk as I spoke.

"What do you mean, Janie?" My dad was sincerely baffled by my comment, but I thought he was just playing dumb.

"I'm way too smart for that, Dad. I got those doctors to believe whatever I wanted them to." My tone was arrogant and sinister. "I didn't even spend a day in there."

My dad really had no idea what I was talking about but went on to find out that the cops had taken me on quite a field trip in an attempt to scare me. They thought that if they could show me what I was in for, I might put down the needle. They obviously didn't know whom they were messing with.

I wasted no time after that getting deeper into a situation that would lead me to some very dark places. When I should've been going to court dates, attending drug counseling sessions, and taking steps toward being a new, sober Janie, I was out shooting and selling, doing what I could to avoid the inevitable. Although I had no regard for my future or the consequences of my actions, my parents had made me their full-time project, and they were doing all they could to keep me from completely ruining my life. The police had called and informed them that I had until a certain date to turn myself in before things got really bad. They were now working against the clock.

My dad knew that he had to get me to the police station, and he was willing to do anything to get me there. He called me one day and told me that something was wrong and he needed to talk to me. Although I was pretty selfish, I did want to know what was going on, so I went home. When I got there, he explained to me what was going on, and we talked about what we needed to do. My dad explained that we would go to post bail before we ever stepped into the jail so I would be out within hours.

I was angry with everyone and didn't really care what he or the police had to say, though. As we sat and I half listened to all my dad had to say, I began to see the seriousness in my dad's eyes. I also began to see something that I felt I had been missing my whole life; I began to see the love he had for me. He was genuinely concerned for me. I was still hurt by a lot of things that I blamed him for, but because I finally found something in him I had been searching for for so long, I agreed to let him take me in.

It's important to realize that this was not a soft moment that led to an emotional breakthrough for me. Sure, I could see that my dad cared, but there was a lot of hate I still harbored, and one moment of sincerity was not going to wipe that out. I still had a long way to go to becoming an emotionally solid person. This experience began to work on the wall I had built up, but I still had quite a chip on my shoulder. I was willing to do this one thing for him, though.

Full of bitterness, I climbed into my dad's car, and we rode silently to the police station so I could turn myself in. My dad stopped to post my bail beforehand so I wouldn't have to spend days or weeks in jail. We arrived at the police station, and I walked in. This time, I was angry more than scared. I knew the drill now, and I wasn't afraid. I would be in and out and back out to my life in no time. I was just going through the motions.

If the first time in jail taught me nothing, the second time I learned even less. I approached it the very same way I had the time before, which meant that I forgot about it the second I was out. The revolving door was now turning.

After I got out, I was on the run from the law. They were tracking me down. By this time, they had all the evidence they needed and all the warrants to arrest me and bring me in. I had already sold to an undercover cop twice, not to mention the several other charges against me. Because of my laundry list of warrants and the fact that I had escaped so many other attempts the police had made to lock me up, they wanted me badly.

Everyone else I ran with had already been busted, and I was the ringleader. Now they wanted me, and they had enough now to get me. They didn't just want me because of my crimes, though; they wanted the information I could provide them. That was not going to happen, though, no matter what the consequences.

There were more arrest warrants out for me than I could have ever imagined (even though I did know I was in a considerable amount of trouble), and I was doing anything but going quietly. I was the last on the list, and the police and DA were not going to stop until I was behind bars. The police were just as sneaky as I was. They needed all the charges to stick, so they waited till they had all their facts before they came after me.

I did not know that my dad was watching out for me while all this was going on. I was in my own little world and had no real contact with either of my parents. In fact, I stayed as far away as I could from them. I had already explained very clearly (and loudly with some vulgarity) that I was not interested in their help, and I had no intentions of going back on my word.

I dodged until I couldn't dodge anymore. One afternoon my dad called me and asked where I was; he told me he needed to talk to me about something important. He came to the Super 8 hotel and said that he got a call about some warrants out for me. He told me that it was pretty serious and that he had found a lawyer whom we needed to go see who might be able to help us.

After realizing the gravity of the situation, I called the secretary of the lawyer to ask what all I was facing. She pulled up the warrants and said there were seventeen warrants and a bond that was one and half million dollars. Upon hearing "one and half million dollars," we began to panic. This was much more than

I was expecting. I knew I was in trouble and that I had done a lot wrong, but I didn't think I had done a million dollars' worth of wrong.

We decided to meet at the attorney's office to see if there was any way he could help. I met my family at the office of the attorney, and I was completely doped up on meth and Xanax. As I drove there, I listened to the Carrie Underwood song "Jesus Take the Wheel." As I drove and listened to the lyrics of the song, I wondered if He would ever take the wheel of my life and fix this broken mess. Would I ever let Him?

The attorney ended up being no help to us. He went so far as to tell my dad to let me rot in jail; ten good, long years would straighten me out he said. At hearing the person who was supposed to have the answer to my problems say that not only could he not help me but that his recommendation was to send me to jail for a decade, I ran and ran hard.

With the attorney's suggestion to let me rot echoing in my head, I stayed in hiding and began to seriously consider leaving the country. I was what one might call a "hot mess." I ran for a couple of months and stayed in hiding, jumping from place to place trying to outrun the law—always trying to stay one step ahead so I didn't get thrown away. I did keep in some contact with my family as I bounced around, but not much. My priority was staying out of jail, after all, not checking in with my parents.

There was one incident while I was running that I have a very vivid memory of. I was sitting in my dark-green Lexus under a towering tree that stood outside my dealer's house. I had just blasted myself with a shot of dope and was all thrown off by it. As I sat blown in my luxury car, I leaned over the steering wheel and said, "God, I'm only existing. I'm not living. I want to live again. Help me to live again."

I meant every word that I said to God that day. My life was a runaway train, and it was about to hit the end of the tracks. I needed help but didn't know what to do to get it. God knew, though, and He heard my prayer that day. An unexpected call came in after that. Be careful what you ask God for because He'll give it to you, but it may not always come in the package that you're expecting or wanting.

My cry for help had been heard. The cops contacted my parents. My dad asked the officer if he would give them time to get me to come in myself and do the right thing. The officer gave my dad his word that he would. In return, my dad gave the officer his word that he would bring me in. I was running away from my problems and letting my parents shoulder the burden. I felt I had dealt with enough in my life. I was finished.

In running from consequences, I was digging myself a hole that was going to completely bury me, and I knew it. Meth, Xanax, and bulimia helped drown that out from time to time, but it was always hanging in the back of my mind, pushing to the front if I let the high wear off for too long. I thought that turning my back to the whole situation would make it eventually go away. That is not how these things work, though. When I turned my back, the monster only grew larger and got uglier. I was running away from the problem, but it had no intentions of running away from me. I was going to have to deal with the consequences of my actions at some point, but I wasn't quite ready to do that.

I decided that instead of facing my fears I would flee the country. I didn't want to man up to the trouble I was in, so I was going to run just like I had run from everything else. It was all I knew how to do anymore. So I had found my solution, and all I had to do was go. Someone knew what I needed more than I did, though, so He sent a not so subtle suggestion to me.

One day as I was driving, heading toward the border to escape my past, my phone rang, and it was my mother. My mother wasn't the type to show the kind of love and affection my father did; she was harder on me, so I rarely ever heard from her.

I always felt like she didn't care about me, but that was never true. She was just hurting and could not stand to see her little girl this way. She gave me tough love. Because my mother was always more reserved with her emotions, when she called and begged me to come home, crying and sobbing, it softened my heart for a split second, and I gave her my word that I would come home and do the right thing. Because I had given my mother my word, days later I returned home. I came with a heart full of hatred, but with boldness I took pride in my mess and did what I had to do.

In July 2006, my mom convinced me that it was time to admit defeat. Being featured on *Crime Stoppers* helped drive that point home. Beyond my television debut, the police had made it very clear that after July

14, I would be in a lot of trouble and wouldn't stand a chance. It was now or never for me, so it was time to go.

Meth wasn't going to solve this one. I had exhausted every possibility and could not come up with an out. I even considered leaving the country to escape my problems. Problems have a way of following you no matter what part of the world you are in, though, and I had to be realistic about my options. Unless I wanted to become a permanent resident of Chihuahua, Mexico, I was going to have to come up with a new game plan.

I finally agreed to go, but I waited until the exact date to surrender. I wasn't going a second before I had to, and I wasn't going sober. I pulled as much dope into a syringe as I knew my body could handle, put the needle in my purse, and told my parents I was ready to go. The ride I took with my dad and mom to turn myself in was full of quiet anger; this trip would soon be bursting with audible hate.

As we started, I was driving my car and my mom and dad followed. Halfway between my parents' house and the police station, I started to panic. I pulled off the road and got out of the car. I couldn't do this. I wouldn't do this. This was way too much for a twenty-two-year-old to handle. I began to second-guess my decision to willingly go to prison. I had been avoiding the law because I knew what waited for me once cuffs were put on my wrists. I knew that I had a million-and-a-half-dollar bond. This had gotten much bigger than me, and I wanted to run away from it all at that moment.

My parents pulled in behind me to see what was going on. I was frantic and pacing on the side of the road, listing all the reasons that I wasn't going to get back in the car and just give myself up. I was in control of my own life. Why should I give someone else the reins now? We were quite a spectacle. There was me, breathless and ranting, and my parents, pleading with me as they tried to talk me down.

"Janie," my dad said, "you have to go right now. We have no choice. We have to keep our word or they'll be coming after you with guns."

My dad's argument was hard to dispute. I really wasn't going to make anything better by running. Finally, my mom convinced me to get in the passenger seat of the car so she could drive me the rest of the way, and I acquiesced.

The drive was one that neither my mom nor I will ever forget. I screamed and cussed and spat at my mother. I let her know exactly how I felt and how she and my dad were the reason that I was even in this place to begin with. I told her that they had made this, that she and my dad had created this monster. I don't believe any of those things now; I may not have even believed them then, but I was mad and I wanted someone to blame. I wasn't going to be the one to take responsibility for this mess, and she was there, so I would make her my scapegoat.

My mom continued to drive regardless of my pleas and demands to turn around and take me home. With every mile that clicked by on the odometer, I became more outraged. I got louder and more vile as we drove, saying whatever I could to hurt my mother; all my demons came out to play. I grew more and more hysterical the closer we got to the police station. I was red-faced and shouting, so consumed with hate that my words were getting stuck in my throat. My muscles were clenched, and my entire body was shaking with rage. The floodgates had opened, and I was holding nothing back.

Driving along the road with a psychotic daughter on methamphetamines, my mom felt helpless. As I seethed and fumed, she cried and prayed. She prayed for me in a way I had never heard her pray before. At one point, she called my aunt to ask her to pray, too. She knew Matthew 18:19 (NIV) by heart: "Again, I tell you that if two of you on earth agree about anything you ask for, it will be done for you by my Father in heaven." My mom wept as she explained to her sister what was happening and then told her to pray, to pray hard and mean it.

Matthew 18:19 does not provide a timeframe, and I was too hardened to accept God's love at that time, so as my mom sobbed prayers, I became infuriated. I slammed my fists and flailed. Finally with only a mile to go to the police station, I hit the unlock button on the door handle, swung the door open, and tried to jump from the car that was cruising along at around forty-five miles an hour. My mom dropped her phone, pulled me in, and started struggling with me to keep me from throwing myself onto the asphalt pavement beneath us. This only made me worse. That must've been the longest mile my mom had ever driven.

Finally we arrived at the police station. The sight of black and white cars and navy blue uniforms enraged me. The police knew we were coming, so they were waiting and ready to arrest me. As I got out of the car, a police officer came and began to cuff me. I stood facing my broken-down parents who had tears streaming down their faces with a police officer behind me. As I felt the metal cuffs click around my wrist, I spit at my parents.

"F—- you." Those were my parting words as I was taken away to find out my fate.

CHAPTER EIGHT

CAPTURED

I was now being taken from the local police station to the county jail. Handcuffed and sitting in the back of the police car, I persisted with my tirade. I didn't care if the guy driving was a cop or not. I was going to give him a strong dose of the hate that I had been carrying around for so long. It didn't take long for the officer to realize I was going to be a handful.

After my initial introduction of profanity and shouts, I finally sat quietly with my head lifted high; I was proud of my accomplishments in crime. I was not ashamed of what I had become. I'm an all-or-nothing type of girl, and I had done it big. I was somebody. All I was looking for was to be noticed, and now I had made my entrance. I had made such an entrance, in fact, that as we drove to the county jail the officer called for backup. By the time we got to county, there were three or four officers waiting for my arrival.

As I was going through the process of being booked, I stayed prideful and kept my mouth shut, but I was also tough and hardcore. I had made a name for myself and wasn't about to lose it. I made my way into the jail with my four escorts by my side. I took pride in the fact they needed four officers to bring me in.

I was booked on five counts; two counts of delivery of a controlled substance, one count of organized crime, one count of forgery, and one count of possession. This wasn't the worst of it, though; I also had twelve counts pending. I had no idea what I would be facing with so much against me.

This was the third time I had gone through the booking process. Again, I had transformed. I wasn't angry this time; I was confident. I stood in front of the camera wearing the same stiff gray jumpsuit I had worn the first time, but I wore that jumpsuit with pride. They told me to face the camera, and I did, with my head held high and a smile fixed on my face. I was probably the most expensive inmate they had in there; sure, they could take my picture.

As I walked to my cell this time, I didn't do it as a frightened rookie who was shocked by the hardened women who sat in the cells; I did it like a pro. The women didn't stare back with curiosity or look past me with indifference now, either. They looked at me with respect. I had pull in that place. People knew my name and what I was about. I came in weighing in at barely one hundred pounds, but there wasn't a person in that place who would touch a hair on my head. I even had a nickname, Platinum, because of the price on my head. I wore my crimes like a gold medal in there, and just four months before I was terrified of jail.

◆❖◆

I had pull in jail, and it didn't particularly scare me anymore, but it was by no means pleasant. I couldn't do drugs anymore, so my body ached from withdrawal. On top of that, I was struggling with bulimia more than ever, and there is no detoxing from that. I started to waste away. My health seemed to decline daily. I was deteriorating so rapidly that I had to be hospitalized on more than one occasion. Things were not going well, and it was going to take some time to get out of this.

I had to spend three months at County while I awaited my hearing. Those three months started to change who I was. I had always been an outgoing person who made anything that was going on a little bit more fun. If I was awake, I was probably smiling. I had a lot of hurt inside me, but from the outside, I was about the most fun-loving person you could come across. That changed a little in jail, though. Although I was outgoing, I became hard too—hard like the women who had shocked me the first time I was in. There is only so long a person can keep a needle in their arm without crossing the line from party girl who sells to hardened criminal. I was slipping to the other side, and I hadn't even been sentenced yet.

I was still very outgoing in jail, but I was hard when I needed to be. For the most part, keeping the same outgoing personality got me places in jail. I knew how to work my charm so that everyone liked me, which gave me pull with the people who could get me what I wanted. Although I knew how to be tough to keep my name and respect, I was a fun person even in jail, and I made my personality work. I learned from the evangelistic field and the drug life to adapt to my surroundings and use my charisma to make good out of whatever came my way. I made lots of friends while in County. The girls would cover for me and watch my back, and I did the same for them.

The way I was able to maintain my usual personality was that I was first hard and made it known that no one was going to use me as a doormat. People knew me whom I didn't even know. They knew my name from the streets, so the second I stepped foot in the jail, I had respect. A lot of my people whom I was involved with were already locked up, so I was comfortable in the surroundings; I was with my friends. Because of that, I could be fun loving and maintain my reputation as hard so no one messed with me.

As the days came and went, though, I started to evolve and adapt to my surroundings even more. You can't make it in jail being the smiling party girl, so I became what I had to; I became tough, and I hid any emotion that I had. I was even becoming violent, so violent that I was put on medication to keep me sedated so I wouldn't injure myself and others. The wall that I had started building around my heart after Jacob left got thicker and sturdier while I was awaiting my hearing. I wasn't *like* one of those women I had seen my first time in jail. I *was* one. Things were only getting worse for me, too.

The entire time that I waited for my sentence was a battle in a lot of ways. One of those battles was, of course, my bulimia. My bulimia was my very first addiction. I had used it to deal with a lot in my life. Being locked up, drugs are not exactly readily available, so I used my eating disorder more than ever to cope with what was going on. My body was not in good shape upon arrival because of the drugs and the bulimia, but in jail it was getting out of control.

Another constant fight I had was against prosecutors who wanted me to tell them about the cartel. It felt like I was being interrogated nonstop. They wanted names, dates, stories; any details they could get, they wanted. I wasn't going to talk, though. I had seen what had happened to people when they talked, and I would not have that happen to me. I'd rather face a prison sentence than that. I could be putting myself and my family in harm's way by opening my mouth, and I wasn't willing to risk that. I also had a bizarre loyalty to the people they wanted me to roll over on. I had taken a kind of silent oath that, no matter what happened, I would not snitch. There was no pride in snitching; everyone knew that. The number one rule of the game is you don't snitch. I didn't honor much in the world, but I honored that.

So I spent three months refusing to talk to prosecutors, just waiting to see where I would go from there. I was being broken down in the process. I didn't know how much more of this I could take, and I still had so much ahead of me. I honestly wondered sometimes if I was going to make it through the whole thing.

Finally in October 2006, I went before a judge to find out my fate. My lawyer was able to get seventeen charges knocked down to two. On those two charges the prosecutor was asking for thirty years on the first count and fifteen years on the second count. After deliberation, the judge looked at me and slammed down the gavel. She sentenced me to a five-year prison sentence on the second count of delivery of a controlled substance. On the first count of delivery of a controlled substance, I received ten-year adjudicated probation with a thirty-year prison sentence if I broke probation. I now knew my fate. I was numb as I walked out of the courthouse that day. I didn't know if I should be thankful that charges were dropped or terrified of the five years ahead of me.

My family, who had been there with me every step of the way, wept as I was taken away once again. My mom and dad were distraught. They had come to visit me at the county jail every opportunity they could. They saw what was happening to me and were terrified that I would not be able to survive any more time behind bars. They had prayed and wept for three months for me, and now I was being taken away again. The state was taking away their baby. With such a grim outlook, it was hard to see that anything positive could be born of my situation. The sentence seemed to both my parents and me like a death sentence.

CHAPTER NINE

BREAKING POINT

After being sentenced, I was taken back to the county jail to wait for my transfer to the big house. I knew that I would be there for a while, so I decided to settle in and make friends because without friends in jail, things can get scary. I made alliances with some and enemies with others. I also learned to show no emotion other than anger and hate to be sure no one would think I was weak. My survival depended on my façade, so I had to work hard to keep it intact.

I was in County for almost four months after my hearing, and I was only getting sicker with the passing of the days. My parents were still visiting me daily, which offered a little comfort, but once visitation hours were over, all my fears and anxieties were there waiting for me.

By the time February arrived and it was time for me to transfer, I was on the brink of a meltdown. My body and mind were destroyed. The bars of the jail cells felt as if they were closing in on me. I realized that people were not meant to be put in cages. This experience was doing me much more harm than good.

Finally, my transfer day came. Although I was only going from one cage to the next, I was ready to be out of that jail. The taste of the food, the smell of the cell, and the feel of the rough county-issued blankets were all things that I would not miss once I passed through the tall chain link fence that was crowned with razor wire. I had no idea as I was being led out of my jail cell and through the inmate exit what kind of hell awaited me.

My journey from county jail to state prison started with a strip search. Although I was becoming used to getting naked in front of prison guards, the experience never seemed to lose its impact; I never stopped feeling like livestock going through inspection at a sale. After the search, I was put in transit and then waited to be classified to a prison unit. I could already tell at that point that the move to state prison was nothing I should have been looking forward to.

After just one week in prison, my health had severely deteriorated. I was so sick and weak that even the inmates noticed that I was in terrible shape. The seriousness of my condition could not be ignored, so after just seven days, I was taken to a nearby hospital for evaluation. I arrived at the hospital, was seen by a doctor, and was sent away for further evaluation within a couple of hours. Because I was so sick, I was hardly aware of anything while I went through all the moves and evaluations. Everything happening seemed so surreal; I felt as if I were watching the situation, not living it. Everything felt far away and detached.

I was taken in a van to Jester Four, a psychiatric ward. That name should sound familiar, because it was described at the beginning of my story. This is the point that I was thrown in a four-foot-by-eight-foot cell, naked with nothing but a blue suicide blanket to keep me warm. This was the point that I began to break down and ask God for help.

Terrified and shivering, I was put in a cell by myself where I had to wait. It was a weekend, so no doctor would be able to see me. I was kept in that tiny cell with no clothes for days. I was skeletal and sick, and the cell was freezing. There was no way to get warm, though, and there was no one to help me. When I had finally had too much, I curled into a ball under the stainless still bunk, and I prayed that God would come to my aid.

I cried out for help with what little strength I had. I asked God to send angels to comfort me. I knew it was a long shot, but I was cold and desperate. Little did I know that God had awakened my parents that same night and they began to pray for me, too. They knew that I was in some kind of danger. My mom asked God to send angels to protect and stand beside me. God heard our prayers, and I felt the wings of angels hover over me, and heat begin to flow through my body. I was never cold again.

The only thing that kept me sane during that time was the Word of God. It became my source of strength. Every scripture I could remember learning as a child came back to me, and I clung to each one of them. I would repeat the scripture in Isaiah 40:31,

> But they that wait upon the Lord shall renew
> their strength; they shall mount up with wings
> as eagles; they shall run, and not be weary; and
> they shall walk, and not faint.

One of those cold, lonely nights as I sat and recited that scripture from Isaiah, an amazing thing happened. The inmate in the cell next to me began singing that scripture in song. As I listened to the voice float through the concrete walls and iron bars, I suddenly knew that God was watching over me and He had not left me there to die.

Within the next few days, I received a letter from my mom. I read the letter again and again; it had become a source of comfort for me and kept me from feeling completely alone. Mom would always end her letters with the scripture in Philippians 4:13, "I can do all things through Christ which strengthens me." Those words gave me strength to keep on going.

I wanted nothing more than to leave the hellhole that I was in. I would count down the days as I would hear the guards walk down the hall. They would count us to make sure we were all there; with every meal and every medicine run I knew how many hours were in a day. I just wanted the day to end and another to begin. I lived my life one day at a time, and every day I made it through was an accomplishment for me.

I kept a peace during that time that was amazing. I began to talk to God again and even to minister to the other inmates about Him. Even though I did not live according to God's Word at the time, it was a step in the right direction. I had, at least, created an open dialogue with God now.

Those twenty-one days in that drafty, lonely cell really made me reflect on my life and the choices I had made. I began to wonder why I had let myself fall so deep into the lifestyle that had led me there. I began to realize that I had a choice every day in what I would do from that point on; I could change my way of thinking or wallow in my self-pity. I chose the former and began to thank God for waking me up every day and for things he had saved me from—like death.

After twenty-eight long days, I was taken from Jester Four to a prison for the criminally insane. My eating disorder was more than a regular prison could handle, so I spent the next seven months in intense therapy sessions and under constant supervision of a doctor.

At first, it seemed that going somewhere that could treat my bulimia would be a blessing for me. As I settled in, however, I began to see that this might not be as helpful as I had hoped. In fact, it seemed that this prison for the criminally insane may have been making my illness worse, not better.

I spent months being forced to eat, which I was not able to do. I wasn't *refusing* to eat; I wasn't *able* to eat. Because my body was so damaged from bulimia, I would involuntarily vomit when anything hit my stomach. I would then have to clean up the vomit. I would say that I, again, felt as if I were being treated more like an animal than human, but not even animals are treated this way. Things seemed to only go from bad to worse. Through all this, I couldn't understand how any of this was supposed to rehabilitate me or help me become a standup citizen. It seemed that being dehumanized would only push me further down the path it was supposed to be taking me off of.

Luckily, though, God gave me favor with the warden of the prison. After the warden saw me locked in a room one day, he asked me about myself, and I told him all about my illness. He took favor in me, and so did the doctor who treated the inmates. They gave me a treatment plan, and I was monitored closely to be sure I wasn't getting worse. I had to weigh in every day.

I was always around ninety-four pounds, so when I got over 105 pounds, both the warden and doctor were proud. They would pull me out of my cell to eat every meal, and they even put me on ensure for weight gain. I couldn't stand that I had to gain weight; it was my biggest fear. I knew that I would have to do it if I wanted to get better and leave that place, though.

Although I did hate a lot about where I was, I did appreciate all that the warden and doctor did for me. The warden not only helped me to become healthier, he allowed my family special visitation. It was a luxury I did not take for granted. I looked forward to every visitation I got. It was my one connection to the outside world and to the life I once had.

My parents weren't the only people to visit. Jeff also came to see me in prison often and always made sure I had plenty of money on my books. Although I know that the two of us had a strange relationship, I thought that it proved something that he even took care of me in prison. Like I said, he was always there to save me.

Along with being allowed special visitations, I also was put in an air-conditioned building, which is more than a luxury when you are locked up, and given my own private cell with a roommate. God gave me a luxurious place to stay—or luxurious comparatively speaking, anyway. He was watching out for me when I needed it most. The place I had come to was more like a hospital than a prison. I saw parole as well while I was in the psychiatric hospital and was hoping I would get to go home.

In September 2007, the state decided that I was well enough to make it in a regular penitentiary, so I was discharged and sent back to the women's state prison to do the remainder of my time. I kept my head down and tried to just keep my sanity while I waited for my release date. I was still battling my bulimia, but I had at least rekindled my relationship with God, so I was making some progress.

On December 31, 2007, I made parole and became a free citizen of the State of Texas once again after serving eighteen months of my five-year sentence. Leaving that prison felt the way the sands of a shore must feel to someone who has just barely escaped drowning. I literally kissed the ground once I was on the other side of the towering chain-link fences that had kept me from my life the last year and a half.

I felt like it was my birthday the day I was released. I couldn't stop smiling or thanking God that I was free again. I made a promise to myself and to God that

I would never return to that nightmare of a place. I didn't think it would be a problem for me anymore. If I could make it through prison, I could surely make it through sobriety.

CHAPTER TEN

THROWING IT ALL AWAY

Sobriety proved to be a little bit more difficult than I had imagined. I found out fast that I had not overcome my addiction; I had only been locked away from drugs. It was easy not to use if there was no way to get dope. On the outside, though, I was surrounded by temptation.

As part of my probation and parole, I had to continue counseling for my eating disorder and my drug problem. I was ordered to attend an outpatient rehab program and also ordered to go to a separate therapy for my bulimia. It felt as if I was being bombarded with treatments, and I began to feel overwhelmed by everything. All of these things were supposed to help me learn to deal with life in healthy ways, but nothing they taught me helped me deal with the stress of the programs themselves. There was only one thing I could think of that might offer some relief, so I went for it.

After only three weeks out of prison, I was right back where I started, but this time it was alcohol and prescription pills that I ran to. I found a group of people to party with so I could pick up where I left off. I didn't just fall into the party scene, either; I plunged into it headfirst. While this was going on, my bulimia was also getting worse. It seemed I was not just backsliding; I was blazing new trails where mistakes were concerned. The promises I had made to myself and God were buried deep down in my consciousness, and the fear of going back to prison was eclipsed by addiction. I had learned nothing from my eighteen months in prison.

My body was taking some heavy abuse now. My bulimia had spiraled out of control so much so that the only thing I kept in my stomach was Jack Daniels whiskey, Xanax, baby food, and apple sauce. I had officially put God back on the backburner and started to do what I could do to replace Him however I could. I tried modeling for a short stint, but nothing came of that, so I went back to old reliable Jeff and partying. I started drinking heavily and did pills because I couldn't shoot dope anymore; I was being drug tested every week. I also couldn't get a good job, which led me back into drug use. I couldn't be a makeup artist anymore or do the things I was good at, so I figured, why not?

My family could see that I was slipping away yet again. This time was even more terrifying than the first because everyone knew it wouldn't be just an eighteen-month stretch I would be sent away for if I messed up again. Everyone but me seemed to be concerned about my future. I was only worried about the now, though. I was working on instant gratification, so consequences weren't on my radar.

Knowing what was in store for me if I didn't clean my act up, my family, especially my grandmother, constantly begged me to go to Teen Challenge, which is a faith-based twelve-month program to help people like me who are struggling with substance abuse. The purpose of Teen Challenge is to look at addiction through a lens of Christianity and help those affected by it to learn to become mentally, socially, physically, and spiritually well. Unlike prison, the program works through love and understanding, not fear and degradation. I wasn't ready for help, though. I wasn't ready to face myself and deal with me. I didn't want to let go of my bitterness and hate. It was all I had to hold on too. I hated myself, and that is why I hung on so long to the things that were killing me. It was better to hate than to hurt in my eyes. Hatred and the abuse I put my body through because of it was destroying me. Unfortunately, my body wasn't able to handle the amount of abuse that I did to it while I immersed myself in my hate.

One afternoon, while waiting tables at the Cotton Patch restaurant, I started to feel off. I figured I was just tired or it was just my body craving more pills. I was less than one hundred pounds now and drank and popped pills daily, so feeling strange was a regular part of my day. I tried to work through the feeling, but it was more than exhaustion I was feeling. Suddenly I knew what was going on; I was having a stroke.

I was going into shock, and I was losing feeling on one side of my body. My mouth was drawing up, and I was drooling out of the side of it. I begin to lose my hearing and went unconscious. The manger called 911, and an ambulance got there and immediately hooked me up to an IV. I was rushed to the local hospital. The doctor said they got me there right in time. Any longer and there would have been permanent damage and I may not have even lived.

I woke up in a hospital with tubes sprouting from my body. When I asked why, it was explained that I had suffered a mini-stroke. I figured so much. I was only twenty-four years old, and I had just had a mini-stroke. Something was going to have to change.

I was in the hospital for a week while I recovered. I gained seventeen pounds from the fluids they gave me, which terrified me. I didn't want to gain weight; if anything, I wanted to lose more weight, so as soon as I was released, I purged and purged until I lost the weight the fluids had made. I was seriously sick, both physically and mentally.

During that time, my parents really pushed Teen Challenge. They couldn't understand why I was doing this to myself, and I really couldn't either. Although I knew I was self-destructing, I didn't know if I was ready to commit to a different lifestyle just yet. I would have to give Teen Challenge and complete life change some thought before I threw in the towel.

When I got out of the hospital, I decided I wasn't ready to hang up my party shoes just yet. I spent months living in the world, staying out all night drinking and popping whatever pills I could get my hands on. It was just so much easier than rehabilitation, or at least I thought so at that time.

It really wasn't a party to me anymore, though; it was a way of survival. The alcohol and pills were my way of numbing all the pain from my life. It was my way of escaping my reality. It wasn't a party; the party was over. It had morphed from a party to a method of masking my hurt and pain. It was the only way I knew how to deal with all my issues. I buried every hurt I had in alcohol and drugs. The problem with that, though, is that one day they make their way to the surface and you have to face them again—when this happens, there is no more running.

I was addicted, and when you're addicted, you have no choice but to continue the cycle, even if you want to stop. There's no way out. Deep down inside me, I longed for a better life that didn't involve alcohol, drugs, or even Jeff, since he was a symbol of the monster I had become, or better yet a symbol of the monster that had consumed me. I just didn't know how to get out. I wasn't sure I had the strength to try.

Once modeling didn't work out for me and the party scene began to lose the little luster it had left, I came to the conclusion that there was only one thing left for me. I was tired of hurting, and I was tired of hurting my family, so in December of 2008, I told my family that I would go to Teen Challenge. I got permission from the parole board, my probation officer, and the judge, so I was set and ready to go. I had one last thing to do before I went, though.

Before I left to become a new person, I wanted to see Jonathan. He had been there for me through so much that I had to see him and tell him good-bye before I left. Even though we would spend long periods without talking to one another in the midst of the craziness that was my life, I always knew I could count on him. He was my anchor and my rock, and I had to see him one last time before Teen Challenge.

Jonathan and I had been talking on the phone for a couple of months before I decided to fly out to see him. Talking on the phone with him, I started to believe that something may actually happen between the two of us—if not emotionally, at very least physically. After countless phone conversations, I made up my mind that I had to see him one last time before I went off to become the new and improved Janie. Because Jeff could see how much this meant to me, he was the one who actually bought the plane ticket for me to go see what may happen with the guy whom I thought may be the man of my dreams.

I got on a plane to see Jonathan with different ideas of how the visit would go. I had loved Jonathan for so long. All I ever wanted was for him to love me back. He always had a girlfriend, though, and I always had drugs and other men, so our relationship could never blossom into anything more than what it was. Things were different now, though. I was going to get sober once and for all. I couldn't wait to tell him about it, but I was going to have one last hoorah before I started my new life of sobriety, so I drank as much as I could as fast as I could as the plane took me to see Jonathan.

When I first stepped off the plane and into the airport, Jonathan was excited to see me. In only took a couple of more steps in my direction, however, for his perception to totally change. He immediately knew that this was not going to be any tearful reunion with hugs and "I love yous." He soon realized that I was extremely sick and drunk. Watching me stumble off the plane at barely one hundred pounds was all it took for his dreams of us being together to wither and die.

He knew I was in no shape to be in a relationship or build a life with him. I was worse than he had ever seen me, and it cut him to the core. He thought that me coming meant that I was healing and ready to be serious about him and about my own life. My off-balance walk and slightly slurred speech made it pretty obvious I was not ready, though.

I stayed for three days with him right after the Thanksgiving holiday, and every moment was chaos. He had just lost his child to a sickness and was in no shape to take care of me. He was grieving over the death of his daughter and facing his own demons at that time. My arrival had only made things worse for him. While he was trying to learn how to live without the person he had loved more than life itself, I was there wasted, making everything a little harder to deal with. The more I drank, the more he pushed me away, and the more he pushed me away, the more I drank. I couldn't stand being rejected by him, and he couldn't stand my addictions. We were in a destructive cycle that was going nowhere.

At the end of weekend, it was time to go home. The whole weekend was a catastrophe. The man I had always wanted love from and expected so much from had turned me away. I got the physical part of the deal but none of the emotional. His rejection hollowed me out in a way I didn't think could be done after all I had experienced. I always hit the highest highs and the lowest lows with him.

So on a Sunday afternoon we drove to the airport. He had rejected me once again. I just wanted to feel loved by him; I wanted him to love me the way I had always loved him, but I found out quickly that wasn't happening. As we were driving on the interstate to the airport, I screamed at him with tears running down my hollow cheeks, "Why can't you just love me? What's wrong with me that you won't love me?"

"You need to get yourself together. Go and get help," Jonathan said back to me. "You're out of control. Maybe someday we could be together but not now, not this way."

His words completely crushed my heart, and I don't think he even cared at the time. He dropped me off at the airport, saw that I made it into the terminal, hugged me, and then turned and walked away. With a broken heart, I headed to the bar to get loaded before I stepped on the plane to numb what had just happened.

I could not bear the rejection and hurt. I got on the plane as drunk as a person could be and passed out. Before I knew it, I was waking up in the Dallas airport where Jeff picked me up and took me back home to our place (I lived with Jeff at the time).

As soon as I got back, I tried to get in touch with Jonathan, but he ignored all my calls. The one thing I had left was gone, and so I didn't care to live anymore. I had lost the last thing I was holding on to. I said, "The hell with it." I stayed in bed and drank and popped pills for days. Jeff was worried about me because he had never seen me this way. I had been to a lot of dark places, but this was the darkest.

I had thought so much about what would happen with Jonathan. The only thing I didn't take into account when I imagined our conversation was that Jonathan may not profess his love back to me, and that is exactly what happened. There was no long embrace or tearful kisses. There was only him telling me that we weren't going to happen. My whole world crumbled. I didn't really care about Teen Challenge, sobriety, or my freedom anymore.

After two or three days back home wallowing in self-pity and full of whiskey and pills, I got the call that would change my life forever. I had missed my appointment the day before, so my probation officer was pretty irritated with me, to say the least. She was looking for any reason to revoke my probation, and she found one. As I drove to my probation, I knew I was going to jail. I had made the amazingly dumb decision to smoke pot, which doesn't leave your system for some time. I had tried to clean my system out, but nothing worked. I was doomed.

On December 2, 2008, I walked into my probation drunk and failed my drug test. I was arrested right there, booked, and taken back to the county jail to await my sentencing. It was like déjà vu. I wasn't angry or confident this time. I was broken.

I was in County for eighteen days while I awaited my trial. I was completely different than I had been the first time I was there waiting to find out my fate. I was hard, really hard. There was no fun-loving Janie left. This time around, I didn't have to pretend to be tough or hide my emotions. I was tough, and I had no emotions.

CHAPTER ELEVEN

THE GAVEL

On December 18, 2008, as I sat on the edge of a stainless-steel bunk bed in my cell, completely quiet and trying to get control of my mind, I heard something outside my cell. The sounds of the jingling keys that hung at the side of a guard that was walking down the corridor caused my heart to jump up into my throat and my chest to tighten around my lungs. I knew they were coming for me. The footsteps became louder as the guard with the jingling keys and another guard made their way toward B-tank, my holding cell.

As the guards approached, I felt like we may have been the only people left in the world, even though I was surrounded by other inmates who were trying to comfort me. I didn't hear their words or feel their presence anymore, though. I could only see the guards who were beginning to look like they were two of the four riders of the apocalypse to me as they unlocked my cell and walked toward me.

A heavyset female guard moved me from my cell to the elevator and downstairs to be shackled and chained. After I had been shackled, I was led down a long tunnel with flickering fluorescent lights that made everything feel eerie and foreboding. I felt that I was doing dead man's walk. I may as well have been. I may not have been going to meet Sparky, but I was going into the courtroom to stand before the judge and find out how much more of my life would be eaten up by this prison.

As I walked down that ominous passageway that was leading me to my fate, for a brief second I wondered what I must have looked like to everyone else. The time I had spent in prison had manifested itself in my physical appearance, from my dead bleached hair with dark-black roots to my skeletal figure that my jumpsuit hung on, one could see the results of prison. I was not the Janie I used to be. Of that there was no doubt.

As I continued down the seemingly endless hall, I was completely disoriented and every thought in my head was bouncing off another as I tried to keep my focus. Chaos had broken out in my mind. All I ever wanted was to make my own choices and control my life, but here I was, bound by the decisions I had made that brought me back to prison a second time. Before the drugs, I wanted to be a pediatric nurse. I had so many dreams and hopes for my life, but all had been shoved behind dope-filled syringes and pill bottles. I should have been in nursing school, but I chose drug wars and a life filled with crime. My thoughts were interrupted when the officer on duty called my name. "Burkett, let's go." It was time.

I knew that my family, along with Bobby and Karen Cook, would be sitting in the courtroom waiting to see me. I felt so much shame in what I had done: lying, stealing, rejecting, and using them. In spite of it all, though, my family was still there to support, love, and fight for me. I finally understood what unconditional love meant. For so long I had felt unloved, but I was seeing what a lie that was now.

I entered the courtroom, chains rattling as I walked. I looked at my family. My heart sank as I saw the pain and sadness on their faces, and I wondered what was going through their minds. Were they resentful for what I had put them through? I had betrayed them and the Burkett name. I knew my parents must have asked themselves a thousand times, "Where did we go wrong? What could we have done differently?" The answer was nothing, though; it wasn't their fault. They were good parents. I was the one who chose this life for myself.

The courtroom was full with other inmates and their families. I kept looking back at my family, so desperately wanting them to hold me and take me home. I knew that was not going to happen, though. I had thrown my life away, and I knew it.

The hearing started, and I braced myself. There were several people before me; some were sentenced to prison, some went home, and others got probation. I sat there wondering what my sentence would be. I had already served eighteen months in prison not even a year ago. I had already been given a chance to change my life, but my addictions were too strong. They had had a death grip on me and weren't letting go. I wondered if the judge was going to give me another second chance or send me back to prison.

After I had watched those before me listen to their verdicts, finally my name was called: "Janie Burkett vs. the State of Texas on the count of delivery of a controlled substance in the first degree." If I had had anything in my stomach, at that point it would've been on the courtroom floor. I could feel the tightening in my chest return and my palms dampen.

The guard came over and escorted me to the front of the room. I stood there beside my lawyer as the hearing started. There were series of witnesses called to testify on my behalf. An assistant women's director at the Teen Challenge Recovery Center in Corpus Christy was the first to testify. She told the judge that the program had a bed open for me and went on to explain how the program worked and the ways it would benefit me.

After the woman from Teen Challenge finished, my dad took the stand. I know it must have broken his heart to look down at me from a witness stand and see the anguish and fear on my face, knowing that I had done this to myself. There was nothing he could do to stop it, though. I realized his pain, and I could feel it myself as I looked into the eyes of my broken daddy. So many times he tried to save me from myself, but I always walked away. He spent so much time and money to get me out of trouble. He just wanted a good life for me, one filled with joy and happiness.

After some time on the stand, my dad stepped down and the hearing continued. I was terrified. I knew my odds of getting out of this were not good at all.

I hoped for a miracle, though, that somehow I would escape and be given mercy.

Finally, the hearing ended and the judge sat there for a few minutes looking over all the testimonies and contemplating her decision. She was about to make a decision that would change my life forever, a decision that would impact my life and the lives of my family for many years to come. Looking at me through her glasses, she said, "I know about Miss Burkett's bulimia and the all the issues she deals with. I understand that she was raped, but that is no excuse for what she did. So I am confining Miss Burkett to the Texas Department of Corrections Women's Prison for the next forty years."

At that moment, I felt my heart stop. Tears began to fall down my face. The life I once knew was gone; it no longer existed. I heard a shout that I recognized as my mother's, and my face began to burn. Forty years? What did that mean? I couldn't wrap my mind around that. That was like…my entire life.

In desperation, I looked back at my family and said, "What do I do now?" They had no answers for me that day, though; no one did. I was in complete and utter shock.

The guard on duty escorted me into a small room where I signed for my sentence with a trembling hand and a broken heart. As we left that room and walked to the elevator, my family was waiting to see me. With tears streaming down their faces, they cried, "We love you, Janie. Don't give up! We will work to get this sentence overturned. Hang in there!" As I got into the elevator, I could hear their sobs. I felt like dying at that moment.

My entire life had just been snatched from me, and I no longer wanted to live. I was completely broken.

I wasn't the only one who was shell-shocked. My whole family felt like they had received a forty-year sentence when the judge announced the verdict. My mom, dad, and sisters left the courtroom sobbing and could barely stand. When they got in their car, my dad laid his head on the steering wheel and sobbed, and my mom was crying in convulsions. Although they were dazed and crying too, my sisters tried to comfort my parents and keep them from having complete breakdowns. I know they must have been thinking they would not live to see me free. Forty years was a lifetime.

I contemplated suicide that day. When I returned to the jail, I stood facing the cylinder block wall as the guards took the shackles from my hands and feet. When the door opened to let me into my cell, I clung to the bars in front of me. I was in complete shock. As I stood in my cell, I was suddenly blindsided by the gravity of what had just happened. I sat and began to digest what was going on. I thought about what "for the next forty years" meant for me. I would be sixty-four when I got out. Sixty-four. When it would be time for me to meet my future husband, get married, and start a family, I would be in prison. When it would be time for me to watch my children have children, I would be in prison. I looked up and saw all my friends in the jail waiting to hear the news.

"So how did it go?" they asked almost in unison.

"I got forty years," I replied, staring forward with blank eyes.

When the words "for the next forty years" finally sunk in, my legs fell out from under me, and I collapsed on the hard, cold concrete floor of my cell. I'm not really sure what happened after that. It was a blur.

When I finally came to, I was on my bunk with my friends next to me. They did everything they knew to comfort me through that terrifying moment. Some gave me cigarettes and pills, some gave me words of encouragement, and others gave me Jesus. God was really what I needed at that time, but I had no faith or hope left for my life. I was out of answers. My stubborn will had led me down a long and hard road—a road I never thought I would go down.

Living in prison was not something I would have chosen for the rest of my life, but I didn't want to be a drug addict either. I started to really understand that the only way to overcome the drugs, alcohol, bulimia, hate, and all the demons that had haunted me all these years was through the power of God. I felt that God was out of reach now, though—so far away that it was impossible for Him to hear me.

CHAPTER TWELVE

A STRANGE ESCAPE FROM DARKNESS

Trying to release all the rage buried inside of me, I grew bitter and began to fight with the other inmates. It didn't matter to me if I was given more time for fighting or even put in solitary confinement. I had hit rock bottom, and I didn't see a way up. One night as I lay on my bunk, I began to wonder if God was punishing me for all of my sins. I wondered if He had finally gotten tired of saving me, so He had washed his hands of me and handed me over to the State of Texas to deal with.

I pondered this for days, until one day when God sent me an answer through a precious lady who had been coming to minister to us in the jail. She told me, "Janie, God has the final say, and it's not over until God says it over." Those were the only words I heard, and they gave me strength to go another day and the will to keep fighting. I began to believe that God was going to do something great for me.

A few days later, I met an inmate named Carrie who was in her twenties when she had been given a life sentence, but she had recently been bench-warranted back from prison for a new trial. She made such an impact on my life. Carrie was a dedicated Christian with a great love for God. She had faith that could move a mountain and love and positivity emanated from her. She was sent to me to show me something I needed to see.

I remember the night we sat on the top bunk in my cell talking about God. She asked me if I knew Jesus as my personal Lord and Savior, and I told her that I was raised in a Christian home but wasn't serving God. We began to tell each other our life stories and how we ended up here. She told me she served the Lord into her teens until things happened that caused her to turn to drugs.

Carrie and I were so much alike; we both had a relationship with God at a young age but turned to the world after being hurt or rejected. I felt a deep connection with her from the day she walked through the gates, and now I knew why. I saw peace and joy in her, and I so desperately wanted what she had. I knew it was God, though, and I wasn't ready to receive Him yet. I had always said that when I gave my life to God, it would be all or nothing.

Carrie and I became great friends in the short time we knew one another. She gave me hope to keep going when I was struggling. I would look at her and say, "If she can live her life behind bars and find peace and happiness, so can I." Little by little I began to turn my eyes toward God, and He began to chisel away at the barrier that I had slowly built around my hardened heart. Carrie had cracked the door to let God come in.

God's love began to fill my heart, and all that hate seemed to be melting away like the snow on spring ground. God was the spring sunshine that was melting away what the harsh winter had left behind. I felt that God was replacing my hardened heart with a loving, beating heart that was no longer shielded from others. I began to feel that Jeremiah 29:11 was written just for me: "For I know the plans for you, Janie, plans to prosper you, and give you hope and a great future."

As I would read over that scripture, my stomach would flutter with excitement and my heart would throb with joy. My life wasn't hopeless anymore. I had heard those words all my life, but they had never penetrated deep down in my soul and move me like they did that day. Hope rose in my heart, and I felt as if I had a future. God had given me something to believe in.

It may sound crazy to have a feeling of renewed hope in the wake of the overwhelming sentence I had just been given, since it was basically a death sentence to me, but I did. As far as I knew, I was going to have to spend the rest of my life behind those bars because I wouldn't lay down my rebellion and listen. God had now allowed me to be put in a place where I would have to listen to Him and rely fully on Him. I no longer had anywhere to run, and this is exactly what I needed.

My mind went back to the time I was in jail the first time. I had just been convicted and sentenced to prison for five years and was sitting on my bunk in my cell letting myself wallow in self-pity. I opened my Bible and my watery blue-green eyes landed on Ephesians 3:13: "Therefore I ask you, Janie, do not lose heart at my tribulations for you, which is your glory." That scripture had always stuck in my head.

Through my times of struggle and suffering, I would remember those words that the Lord spoke to me that day, which was strange because I was doing all I could to escape the Lord for a very long time. Since I was in prison with a forty-year sentence hovering over me, I kept those scriptures close to me and knew that even though the devil had tried to destroy me, God would turn this to good in my life and use it for His glory. He may have to do it in prison, but prison is no obstacle for God.

It was very hard to keep faith through the whole ordeal, but I knew that somehow God would take care of me; the overwhelming sentence was all just a part of the plan. He knew what it would take to break me and to bring me to a place of complete surrender to Him. Before this happened, I was unfathomably stubborn and set in my ways. My heart was so full of pride and rebellion toward God and anyone who represented God that He could not work on me. I had to be right there right then to find Him. He had been trying to get my attention for years, but I was too stubborn and foolish. Stuck behind prison bars, though, He finally had my attention!

I could finally see how much I was like Jonah from the Old Testament. God called Jonah to go to the city of Nineveh to speak truth and call the wicked people to repentance. However, Jonah refused to go and ran from the call of God. Because of his disobedience, God sent a great tempest to get Jonah's attention; He even caused a big fish to swallow him. I could now relate to Jonah. This forty-year prison sentence was definitely my great big fish.

I was at last learning that when God tells us to do something, we'd better listen. I was chosen many years ago to be a witness and to share the love of Christ to this generation. I had so much compassion for less fortunate people; I wanted to show them the love of Jesus by helping them. But when I was twenty, I said no to God and ran as far as I could away from Him. I wasn't about to change my lifestyle—the parties, men, sex, drugs, and alcohol. I was a modern-day Jonah running from the call of God. He had called me as a young child to be a voice of hope for the lost and hurting; however, my pain and the lies of the enemy caused me to lose my hunger for God and my will to help people. If I had only said yes to God and followed His ways, I would not be sitting in that lonely jail cell with the reality of spending the next forty years in prison. My hindsight was more than twenty-twenty at that point.

I knew that it was running from God that had gotten me into all the trouble I was in, but I couldn't do anything to change my past. All I could do was focus on my future. I knew that things wouldn't be easy. People are sent to prison as punishment for good reason because prison is one of the last places on earth you want to be. I had messed up, though, in a colossal way, so prison is where I would be for quite some time. I decided I might as well start making the best of it and doing what I should have been doing all along. That crack that Carrie created was beginning to widen, and God was making a full return to my life.

CHAPTER THIRTEEN

EXTRAVAGANT HOPE: WAITING FOR A MIRACLE

Something I should mention is that while in prison, I was also still on parole for my previous prison sentence. Texas law states that if you break your probation, you also break your parole. Because of this law, I could have been looking at three more years. My parole officer scheduled a hearing with the parole board to see if they would revoke my parole and require me to serve the rest of my sentence before I started the new one. That meant that if they sent me back to serve out my original time as well, then I would end up with forty-three years all together. Part of me really didn't care. Three more years didn't seem like too much when I was already facing forty.

I was quite lucky in that my parole officer was extraordinarily good to me. A lot of people who work as parole officers tend to become jaded or lose compassion because of how many cases they see of people like me; not mine, though. Concerned for my well-being, she did what she could to find help for me while I was incarcerated. She also came to see me in jail, and we sat in that little visitation room and talked about what had happened and what the next step would be. She wasn't just going to leave me.

Later I met with the parole attorney who had been assigned to discuss my case and explain what options I had. He was a bit less optimistic about my case than I had hoped. He told me that my parole would be revoked and I would have to serve out the rest of the three years, but it was protocol to have a hearing. He said it would be a miracle if the parole board reinstated my parole. As soon as the attorney told me this, I called my parents to break the devastating news. We were discouraged but still hoped for a miracle.

My parole hearing was set for January 8, 2009, at around 9:00 a.m. The night before the hearing I had an overwhelming feeling that something was about to happen. There was a deep-seeded dread within me that told me I wasn't going to get any breaks. I called my mom that evening.

"Mom?" I asked as I heard someone pick up the phone.

"Hey, baby," my mom replied. Every time I called my parents their voices were a strange mixture of joy and anxiousness.

"I've got a feeling, Mom. I've got a really bad feeling," I said into the receiver.

"About what, hon? Don't get worked up. You just pray. We're going to be there, and so is God, so pray and be patient. There's nothing worrying can do anyway," my mom assured me, but it wasn't helping.

"I can't help it, Mom. There is something on the horizon. Something big is going to happen. I don't know what, but I can feel that something is going to happen."

Our conversation went on that way until the minutes ran out. I insisted something was going to happen, and my mom told me not to fret over and over; then we said our good-byes. I hung up the phone with a heaviness in my gut that told me something was wrong. With nothing else left to do, I crawled into my top bunk and fell asleep.

Around 4:00 a.m., I was awakened by the officer calling my name, "Burkett, What's your ID number?"

I crawled down from my bunk, wiped my eyes, looked through my cell bars, and gave her my ID number. I asked, "What's going on?"

"You're pulling chain," she responded quickly. "Back to prison."

"What?" I asked, trying to get my bearings. "I can't be pulling chain! I have a parole hearing today."

"I don't know anything about a hearing. I'm just doing what I'm told. Your name is on the list to be transferred to the women's prison," the guard said as she handed me a bright-yellow jump suit and told me to get dressed.

"Get dressed," she demanded. "I'll be back in a few minutes to get you."

I stood there in shock. I shouldn't be going back already; I hadn't even gone to my hearing yet. Reality was beginning to really sink in as I slipped into the neon prison jumpsuit. I was headed back to the place from which I had just come a year ago, and that place was going to be my future for a while. With a heavy heart and tears streaming down my face, I stepped into the bright-yellow suit and buttoned it up. It was like I was putting on my misery and shame.

We took the elevator down to the booking area and the guard booked me out. I was dreading going back to that hellhole; I knew what awaited me there. I had no choice, though. I had a lot of choices before, but now I had none. I took a deep breath and prepared myself for what was ahead of me. When the guard clerk was finished booking me out, she put the shackles on my feet and escorted me out the back door to the county jail police car. I got in, and we headed for the Plain State Women's Prison. So this was it.

I fell asleep during the three-hour drive to the prison. I awoke to see the fenced area as we drove down that long driveway, headed for the back of the prison. There I was again; just a year ago I was kissing the ground on the other side of this fence, promising I'd never return. I couldn't do it, though. I was given another chance, but I couldn't do it, so there I was. My poor decisions had led me right back.

My life seemed to only be getting worse. "When it rains, it pours," and for me, it was pouring. I was drowning in all the winds and waves of the great storm. I wondered how Jonah felt when he was thrown into that sea. It had to have been something like this. Did he regret the day he said no to God and turned his back on Him? I know I certainly did. As I rode silently shackled in the backseat of the car and stared out at the prison before me, it seemed that it really couldn't get any worse. All hope was gone. I suddenly remembered the words spoken to me weeks earlier: "It's not over until God says it's over." Even when man says there is no hope for you, God says, "I have a plan for you and your hope is in Me."

The guard who had been with me since that 4:00 a.m. wake-up call was kind to me as we moved through the process. She assured me that my life wasn't over and that there was still hope, even in prison. Although she was the one bringing me back to that hell called prison, I found a strange comfort in her.

She helped me out of the car and walked me into the back door where the guards were waiting for me, then released the chains from my hands and feet and gave my papers to the office guards. After that, she walked away. I felt so alone at that moment.

I stood up against the wall and waited to go through the motions yet again. The new female guard instructed me to get completely naked and put my clothes in a garbage can. I did as I was told. I stood there completely broken, terrified of what was to come, and embarrassed as the guards made comments about my body that was only flesh-wrapped bones at that point. The woman guard gave me a detailed strip search; with a flashlight, she looked between my legs, under my breasts, in my mouth, behind my ears, and at the bottoms of my feet.

Afterward, I was given a white jump suit and was told to take a shower and sit in the holding area until the paperwork was completed. I was then given a brown paper sack with a couple of sandwiches inside of it, but by that time I had lost my appetite.

God gave me the strength to walk through that overwhelming experience. If it weren't for His grace, I wouldn't have made it. The grace of God is so overwhelming; it is boundless and never ending. Even with God's grace protecting and comforting me, though, there were times I really felt as if I was going to lose my mind. I just wanted out. I imagine that Jonah felt the same way. He wanted out of the fish's belly. Well, I wanted out of that prison, the great fish God sent to swallow me up until I would listen and say yes to Him. Just like the giant fish, prison was what God needed to use to show me His grace. It was the blessing that seemed like a curse in the beginning.

After hours of waiting, I was sent to the Transit Unit Block C where I waited for weeks to be classified to a prison unit. When I walked into the unit, I saw two stories of fenced-in cages that looked like dog kennels. As I stared at the kennels and heard the chaos of the other inmates around me, I was reminded once again that "it's not over until God says it over."

Again I returned to Jeremiah 29:11: "For I know my plans for you," says the Lord. "They are good and not evil to give you a hope and a future." Those words burned in my mind and moved my soul. I knew that they were written for me right then. As the words from Jeremiah ran laps round my brain, I had a great revelation within my spirit that God had a plan for me and He would deliver me out of the fish's belly.

I hit a breaking point and did just as Jonah had done; I cried out to God for his deliverance and for mercy. I cried out to the living God for mercy to be given a second chance. With my face buried in my mattress, I repented of my sinful ways and asked Jesus to be my personal Lord and Savior. I promised God that I would dedicate my life to His service and to be a voice of hope to the entire world. I pleaded with God to set me free and to overturn the sentence and send me to Teen Challenge where I could find hope and healing to become the woman He planned for me to be. If not, I asked for His grace to be with me as I served my time in prison. At that moment, I felt like a different woman. God had placed a hope in me that everything would be okay no matter the outcome. That day God gave me the faith to believe He would deliver me.

CHAPTER FOURTEEN

WAVING THE WHITE FLAG

When I was a young girl, I sometimes watched old war movies. It seemed both sides would fight endlessly for days, even months, until one side decided it couldn't fight any longer, so the white flag was raised in surrender. That reminds me of how we are with God when we decide we are just too tired of fighting the war within ourselves. We just wave the white flag and surrender. The best thing I ever did was wave that white flag. I had been fighting for years, and I know that I lost pieces of myself—pieces I may never get back. I think if I had only waved the flag sooner then maybe those pieces would still be intact, but then again, I may have had to go through all I did so I could be an example for others, just as Jonah was for the men on that ship. It isn't always easy being a Jonah, though.

As I sat in my prison cell, I couldn't help but think of all the things I had done that led me to where I was. I knew I couldn't live in the past, though. I had to move forward and let God pick up the remaining pieces and make something better. Even though I was going through one of the hardest times in my life, I chose to believe for my deliverance. God was slowly removing the blinders off my eyes so I could see Him in a much clearer way. It wasn't easy to sit in that cell day after day wondering what the final outcome would be, wondering if I was going to make it. With my illness becoming worse, I felt as if I had no chance of survival, especially with the poor conditions of the prison. The unit didn't even have heat or hot water, so I took ice-cold showers every evening.

I was given two oversized white button-up jumpsuits to wear that swallowed my eighty-four-pound frame. I wore both of them at the same time to keep from freezing in that cold cell. I had no feeling in my feet or hands; I had to keep two pairs of socks on just to stave off the kind of numbness you feel when you're a kid walking through deep winter snows. I wasn't making snow angels, though, and there would be no hot cocoa or warm fire to return to. The kind of cold I felt in prison was relentless, and there was no way to escape it.

The eternal cold caught up with me, and I became sick; all the while my eating disorder was slowly killing me. My body had forgotten what to do with food but hadn't forgotten that it needed it. I was so hungry it hurt, and I would inhale all the food on my tray, even though I knew I would be hugging the toilet minutes later. I was basically starving myself to death, but now it was almost involuntary.

In prison, it seems you are walking nonstop—hiking to the cafeteria, to the yard, to the visitation cell. I hated this because it meant I had to leave my cell, and I didn't like to go out of my cell much. I could feel the stares and hear the whispers as I passed; guards and inmates talked and snickered about me; among the nasty outbursts were suggestions that I was an AIDS patient. It was grade school all over again, but this time I was too thin. I just couldn't win.

All the sneers and insults left scars on me; they all hurt, but I couldn't show it. I had to be tough. The women mocking me as I passed had no idea what I went through every day with my illness, so how could they judge me? I chose to let it roll off my bony shoulders, though. With every disdainful insult, anger gnawed a little more at me, and there were times I wanted to show it, but I didn't want to blow my chances of leaving this hellhole, so I chose to let it go. I would just turn to God and ask him to be with me as inmates and guards tore me down. I had to remember Psalm 27:2(NIV), "When evil men advance against me to devour my flesh, when my enemies and my foes attack me, they will stumble and fall," as hateful words were thrown my way.

There were six women, including me, in my cell, so we all had to work at getting along and staying out of each other's way. Luckily, we all got along well. The women in my tank were a constant encouragement to me; they would not let me forget that things would get better. My cellmates became kind of like family, and they watched out for me; they were even concerned about my health. I met some good women behind those bars who were generous and kind—they just made bad decisions that led them to prison, just as I had.

I was especially encouraged by an older woman in my cell who read the Bible with me. She talked about the trials and testing that Job went through and how he never turned his back on God. Listening to that woman talk about Job gave me strength. I had always known the story of Job, but God sent it to me through that woman when He did to show me what He is possible of and what I am able to get through. I knew God gave Job the same kind of grace He bestowed upon me the day I gave my life to Him. I knew without a doubt God was working on my behalf and would open the iron gates that imprisoned me. I believed with all my heart that my shackles and chains would one day fall to the ground. Through discussing the story of Job with that amazing woman, God had given me a special peace within my spirit. I put all my trust in Him.

I waited with anticipation for Sundays to arrive; we all did. On Sundays we found our peace and strength to go another week. I remember one Sunday in particular when a man came to the prison to minister. He had been in prison multiple times for different things but was now living for the Lord and preaching the gospel. I can't remember everything that was said that day or even his sermon, but I do remember how I felt as I walked back to my cell. I felt as if I was already free. I left his sermon claiming my freedom.

While I was trying to find my peace in prison, my family was back home sick with worry and out of their minds with grief; they had a hard time with the sentence and refused to accept it. They were determined never to give up on me. My mother was tormented every day by the thought of me never coming home. She was terrified that I would die in prison. She was struggling as much as I was with my sentence.

My parents knew that I did not belong in prison, and so they never gave up on me or the hope that I would somehow get out. They had been with me through so much, and they weren't about to abandon me now. As soon as I was sentenced, my parents started calling every attorney they could to ask for help with my case. They contacted seventeen different attorneys looking for someone who would pick up the case and ask for a hearing for a new sentence.

With every phone call, my parents met a new disappointment. One attorney after another refused the case with the argument that I had signed away all my appeals in the first trial. They said that it was almost unheard of to get a district judge to overturn another district judge's sentence. On one occasion, an attorney even told my parents that he had seen a sentence like mine overturned only once in fifty-five years in the State of Texas. Almost everyone my parents talked with told them they were asking for the impossible. That did not stop them, though; they were determined to save me from a lifetime of white jumpsuits and cement walls.

Although both my mom and dad were believing for a miracle, my mom couldn't help but fret over my well-being while they awaited one. My mom would get to the point she could hardly function she was so eaten up with worry. One day, though, God spoke to her with the scripture Philippians 4: 6-7:

> Be anxious for nothing but in everything by prayer and supplication with thanksgiving let your request be made known unto God, and the peace of God which passes all understanding shall guard your hearts and mind through Christ Jesus.

This scripture was my mother's sanctuary, her saving grace. From then on she refused to accept defeat. If God had not shown Himself to her and given her hope, I believe she would have lost her mind. Through this traumatizing time, my parents were surrounded by prayer and love from their friends and church body, though, and they had prayers going up all over the country for me. I knew there were thousands of people lifting me up in prayer.

After well over a dozen nay-saying attorneys and weeks of prayers, my parents finally got the call they had been waiting for since I had been sentenced. My previous attorney, Robert C. Perkins, Jr., contacted them with the news that the judge who had sentenced me had resigned and a new judge was brought into office. He also told them that he would take up my case and petition the judge for a new hearing. God was starting to move.

Although I was learning to trust God again, and I knew He was with me, my flesh still did what it could to torment me. Anxiety filled my heart as I sat every day waiting for some kind of news. I knew that Robert was working endlessly for me petitioning the new judge for another hearing. All we could do at that point was pray and leave it with God; only God could do the impossible.

I know there were days that my parents felt like it was hopeless, days they were discouraged, but they refused to give up. Parents and spouses, I encourage you to never give up on the person you love and are fighting for. Keep loving and praying for them; they will come out on the other side. If my parents had thrown in the towel after eight, nine, ten, and so on attorneys told them no, I would have never made it. I believe in the power of prayer; so keep praying and believing for your miracle.

I had no idea what was going to come of the situation, but I was hopeful that God would turn things around. Deep within me I knew that God wouldn't fail me; He had my back. I may not have understood everything that was going on, but I had a peace within my soul that I can't explain.

I chose to believe that prison would not be the final outcome; I believed I would rise up and escape my horrible fate. I chose to focus on Jesus and not on my circumstances. I was reminded of the disciple Peter who stepped out in faith and walked on water. As long as he kept his eyes on Jesus, he was safe, but when he took his eyes off Him and looked at the winds and the waves, doubts set in and he began to sink. As long as I kept my eyes on Jesus, stepped out in faith, and believed, I knew I would make it through this. I have learned that as long as my focus is on Jesus and not my circumstance, it is much easier to face the winds and waves in my life. I have to remember Jesus is walking on the water with me.

Every evening around 8:00 p.m. the guards would walk the hall screaming, "Mail," and then call us to the front of the cell to pass it out, and every evening I waited for the letter to come that would ease my fears. I received a letter from my mother almost every night. She wrote to encourage me in the Lord. Her letters let me know that everything was going to be fine and that there were thousands of prayers going up for me. She also encouraged me to keep my faith and not to give up. I would cry through most of her letters, wishing I had listened to her when she warned me this would happen. However, I knew God could change my circumstances and put me back on the right track somehow.

Have you ever been in a situation that you just knew things were going to work out? After reading my mom's letters, I was encouraged in the Lord and would wipe my tears and hold my head up. I just knew things were going to be better. It's hard to explain the feeling that is way deep down inside that says, "You're going to make it." I believe that is the Holy Spirit speaking into our spirits to comfort us in the time of need. Each one of us has a knowing inside: that place where we just know that our life is in God's hands and He will make good out of our bad situation. I clung to that place.

Finally one day after the guard yelled, "Mail!" my wait was over; I received the letter that would change my life. I took the letter with my mom's handwriting across the front of it and a stamp with the Liberty Bell on it stuck to the top right-hand corner and crawled into my top bunk to see what my mom had to say that day. I tucked my pretzel stick legs under my skeletal body, licked my lips, and slid my fingers beneath the envelope flap. I pulled out the piece of notebook paper, and my eyes scrolled the words. As I read the letter, my heart stopped. Was this really happening?

The letter read that Judge Christy Kennedy had agreed to give me a new hearing. I would be bench warranted back to county jail. Praise God!

I jumped up and shouted while my heart was pounded against my rib cage. Happiness swelled inside me; it was so intense I could physically feel it, and it felt like I was about to burst from it. God was giving me another chance. I know it was because He saw my heart; He knew I had dedicated my life to His service and would do whatever He asked of me.

I was so excited, but it wasn't over yet. I knew I would have to face my past again, and I still had a fear of the final outcome. I was getting a second hearing, which was definitely a good thing, but that didn't necessarily mean I would get out of prison. I didn't know what the outcome would be, but I knew God was in control, and I had confidence that He was going to deliver me.

The Holy Spirit brought 2 Timothy 1:7 (NIV) to my mind: "For God hath not given us a spirit of fear but of power, love and a sound mind." This is the scripture that brought comfort to me when I felt fear rising in my heart. The Word of God is alive and brings hope and strength in a hopeless situation.

For so many years I hated God, but now I had to trust Him as I never had before. God had finally brought me to a place in my life in which I would listen to His voice and follow Him, and that is what I did; I sought Him diligently and never took my eyes off Him after so much time of running away. I guess God knew all along that it would take something as intense as a forty-year prison sentence for me to die to my own will and enter into fellowship with Him. When the judge first uttered the words "the next forty years," I thought my life was over. I had no idea that it had really just begun. God did though. He knew exactly what He was doing that day in the courtroom. I saw it as Him abandoning me once again, but what He was doing was offering me salvation.

You may think that God has forgotten about you in your fight of life, but I am here to tell you that He has not. He will move on your behalf and break down the walls in your life; He knows how to get your attention. Believe me, I thought God did not know how to talk to me, but I was wrong; He knew exactly what to do to get my attention. I had to suffer a storm and be thrown out to sea for the decisions I had made, but God finally sent me my big fish.

CHAPTER FIFTEEN

MIRACULOUS ESCAPE

In January 2009, I received that fateful letter that proved to me what God was really capable of doing if you let him. There I was in that cell with the news I might be given a second chance. What would I do with it? Would I squander it, or would I take my life more seriously and do what God had been asking me to do for years? What do you do with the chances God gives you? Do you squander them, or will you choose to make good out of what you have been given? God gives us many chances to do the right thing, but I believe that most of us take them for granted. We need to realize that one day we may wake up and will have run out of one more chances. I did realize that while I sat on my cold, steel bunk and reread the piece of paper in my hands. If God decided I deserved this chance, I was not going to throw it away like I had the last one.

I had been given every opportunity to make something of myself, but I chose to keep gambling with my life and making one bad choice after another until I had gambled my way into the state penitentiary. When I was first sentenced, I resigned to the fact that I had *un*made my bed, and it was time for me to lie in the mess I had created for a very long time. Thankfully, God had other ideas and had one more chance left for me. The enemy had convinced me I had used up my chances, but I hadn't; the game wasn't over yet. I promised Him that I would play this one wisely because I realized that it was probably my last one. That one more chance was my new hearing—a new chance at the life God wanted for me.

For days I sat waiting for a county officer to come and transport me back to the courthouse for the hearing. Every day after I read the letter seemed to drag longer than the day before. I curled myself in a tight ball huddled in a nest of blankets and clothes I used to try to stay warm and waited to hear the guards call my name. Finally on January 28 at around 1:00 p.m., I heard the female guard say, "Burkett, pack up your things. You're leaving on bench warrant." Those were the sweetest words I'd ever heard spoken in that prison.

I immediately jumped up and threw only the things I needed in a white mesh bag, leaving most of my food and hygiene items for the others to share. I just wanted out, even if it meant leaving everything behind. I walked down those long stairs, saying good-bye to all the wonderful women I had encountered there; some were happy, others were sad, but they all wished me well.

I walked with excitement down the hall through all the locked doors, pushing button after button so the doors would release. When I reached the back of the prison where the female guard was processing all the new inmates, I looked up and saw the officer who would transport me back to face my new hearing. I was very fond of the officer; she was always friendly and understanding and treated me like a human being. She didn't talk down to me like most of the other officers. She was waiting for me with chains in her hands. I gave her a smile and said, "Officer, so good to see you."

"Same here, Burkett," she said back to me. "You've lost more weight. Have they been feeding you in here?"

"I'm okay. Just happy to be going home," I replied with the first real smile that had been on my face in some time.

Before I could leave the prison, the female officer on duty took inventory of the things I was leaving with, and she warned me that I was not allowed to bring anything back to the prison when I returned.

"That's okay because I am not coming back," I said, looking back at the officer with a new air of self-confidence. "God is going to deliver me."

"You're not coming back? What was your sentence?" she asked in response to my matter-of-fact statement.

"I have a forty-year sentence, and I am going back for a new trial," I said.

"You'll be back."

The female guards standing there laughed at me and looked at me the way adults look at kids when they tell them that they have super powers. They didn't know what I knew, though. They couldn't see yet what faith could do. I wanted to tell them that I had spent my three days in the belly of the big fish, and it was time for me to head out and preach repentance, but I knew that they would still not get it yet. They would, though.

I walked out of those doors with my heavy bag that was almost as big as I was over my shoulder. With my head held high, I had a revelation that those guards were wrong, that I would not be back. I looked up at the blue sky and said, "I am a Burkett, and we are not quitters. I believe in the name of Jesus that I will not be back." I said it, and I meant it. I knew God was going to show me what He was made of. Yes, a part of me was terrified, but I had to believe, even if it felt impossible. God tells us that we need only to believe for our miracle and He does the rest; He is a miracle-working God.

The officer I liked so much seemed reluctant as she put the chains on my hands and feet, which almost didn't stay on because I was so thin. We made small talk as she escorted me into the county jail van, which would take me on the several-hour-long trip back to the county jail. During that drive I felt relaxed and chatted with the officer about how happy I was to be going home, and she asked me if I had been treated well while in prison. It was strange to have someone ask me something like that. I had spent a lot of time having guards bark orders and humiliate me. It felt so nice to be treated so well.

When we arrived back at the county jail, I couldn't believe I was back; just hours before I was sitting in prison serving my sentence. I stumbled out of the van in my chains and took a deep breath. I walked through the back door of the jail with my favorite officer, where I sat on the bench in the booking area. I had to wait for the transfer papers to be processed.

For several hours I waited on that bench with all the others who were being booked for their crimes. There were people being booked for DUIs, drugs, traffic violations, hot checks, child support, etc. As I watched the others, I was struck by how many people passed by me. I thought about how some were probably seasoned pros, but others were first timers who were there because they made that one mistake and they got caught. They were probably terrified just like I was my first time in.

After going through the standard processing routine of waiting, showering, changing into a beige jumpsuit, and more waiting, I was assigned to a cell to await my hearing. There were seven other women in my cell, most waiting to be moved to the state or federal prison. We all had something in common: we had all made terrible choices. As I sat there for hours, talking with some of the others, I knew that God had brought me back here for a reason; I wasn't sure what it was, but deep down I had a peace that He wanted to take the messy life I had been living and turn it into a miracle.

For the next two days I waited for the answer that would change my life one way or another. I was learning to wait on God; everything was in His time, not mine. He knew what the final outcome would be. He is an all-knowing God. The only thing I knew was that my life had changed completely; no doubt about it, I was a different person.

After a restless forty-eight hours, the time had finally come. The new day was here, the day that would change my life forever. When I opened my eyes that morning from a deep sleep, I realized that I had a sweet peace within, although I was also quite nervous for fear of the unknown. My life was in the hands of someone else, and her decision would be my final outcome.

Around 2:00 p.m., the female officer escorted me in chains through the tunnel under the jail to the courthouse. With my head held high and my chains rattling, I walked through the tunnel quoting Palms 23:

> The LORD is my shepherd; I shall not want. He maketh me to lie down in green pastures, He leadeth me beside the still waters, He restoreth my soul: He leadeth me in the paths of righteousness for His name's sake. Yea, though I walk through the valley of the shadow of death, I will fear no evil: for Thou art with me; Thy rod and thy staff they comfort me. Thou preparest a table before me in the presence of mine enemies: Thou anointest my head with oil; my cup runneth over. Surely goodness and mercy shall follow me all the days of my life: and I will dwell in the house of the LORD forever.
>
> KJV

I recall hearing about the Christians in ancient Rome who were thrown into the lion's den for sport to be eaten. They would sing Scripture to bring them comfort as they walked into the death chamber. The Word of God is living and brings peace like nothing else; it gave those martyrs strength and courage, and it is still as powerful today as we walk through trials in life. Saying Psalm 23 over and over gave me the strength I needed and lifted my spirit as I walked that long tunnel.

We eventually reached the courtroom. The courtroom officer pointed to a bench and told me to have a seat. I quickly realized that the courtroom looked empty. There were no other inmates in the room; it was a private hearing. The only other people there were the officers of the court, the court reporter, and my probation officer sitting at the table with the district attorney.

Out of the corner of my eye I saw the door open and watched as my family and Mr. Perkins entered the courtroom. Up to that moment I was getting a little worried, but now everything seemed to grow brighter; seeing them made my day. Dad and Mom had a smile on their faces that gave me warmth and comfort. From the look of it, I knew they were convinced that everything was going to be okay. Their faith was in God, and they believed He wasn't going to fail us now. My mom, dad, and two sisters, Faith and Rebekah, quietly took their seats. Other friends also came to lend their love and support to our family.

My attorney motioned for me to come to the front of the courtroom. As I approached the table, I felt as if my stomach was in my throat. I was so nervous; my life was in the balance, and I knew it. I wasn't sure what was going to become of me, but I had to trust in what I couldn't see.

I made my way to the table where my lawyer and I would be standing to plead my case—plead for mercy. Robert and I chatted for a moment about the case; I can't remember all that was said, but I do remember that he was hopeful. A few minutes passed, and we heard the officer of the court say, "All rise. The Honorable Christi Kennedy presiding." In her long black robe, deep-dark hair, and frame glasses, the judge stepped up to the bench and took her seat. I looked at her and wondered if she would have compassion, even though I didn't deserve it.

The District Attorney agreed that my sentence needed to be reduced, but he wanted the judge to sentence me to five years in prison. However, my attorney, Mr. Perkins, began pleading my case to the judge. He asked her to consider allowing me to attend Teen Challenge rehab for help, or if that wasn't possible, to reduce my sentence to five years and put me into a medical facility for treatment. He argued that if I was to be put back into the prison without medical treatment, I would be dead in six months; at eighty-four pounds, I looked as if I were close to death.

At that point, I believe the judge saw something within me that I couldn't see; she saw someone who wanted to live but didn't know how. I stood there wondering how this would end. I was hoping for a happy ending, but there was no guarantee. Judge Kennedy asked me a couple of questions, and I answered them to the best of my ability. As I look back, the day was somewhat foggy, but I remember feeling that this was my last chance.

My family and friends were in the back of the courtroom listening quietly during the testimony. When my probation officer took the stand, she recalled how, while on probation, I had tested positive for alcohol and marijuana the day before I had been ordered into rehab. With those words, I hoped and prayed that the judge would have mercy and allow me another chance.

Before the judge made her decision, she asked me if I had anything to say. I asked the court to forgive me for all the things I had done in my previous life, and I said I was truly sorry. I knew that I ruined the lives of many people and that my actions were not acceptable. After this, the judge said she would take some time to make her decision.

At that moment my world stopped. As I watched her walk away to her chambers, the anxiety I felt was overwhelming. I had to wait for the answer that would determine my fate. I had no idea what she would say when she returned. I knew that God would be the one to make the final decision.

"I think there's a chance she will send you to Teen Challenge," Robert whispered when he saw my face. As he walked to the back of the courtroom to talk with my family, I felt a peace that I would be okay no matter what happened.

The half hour we waited for the judge to return seemed like days. When she finally took her seat and began to speak, her words rang loud and with force.

"This was a hard decision because of the crime and how large the sentence was. Miss Burkett, if I could, I would give you a sixty-year sentence and probate it because your behavior was unacceptable with the Court. However, that would not be compassionate nor would it be merciful, so here is what I am going to do." As she said those words, I braced myself once again. "I am going to confine you to the Texas Department of Correction for ten years with a ten thousand dollar fine. However, I am going to probate that sentence with the stipulation that you attend the Teen Challenge program and complete it.

"Miss Burkett," she added after a slight pause, "you have been given a second chance. Make something of it."

"Thank you for the chance you've given me. I promise you won't regret this. I will make something of myself," I said, looking at the judge with tears in my eyes.

"This was divine intervention," my lawyer leaned over and said as I looked back at my family.

At that very moment, I had received mercy, mercy like I had never known or felt. My life had just been handed back to me; a new life was about to start.

I lifted my shackled hands up and put them over my face and cried. Then I looked over at Robert Perkins, Jr. with an eternal smile and said, "Thank you."

He smiled back and said with a grin, "If you get into any more trouble, don't call me."

My family was overjoyed; their baby girl was free. Their prayers had been answered. God had just shown us His mighty hand, holding high the white flag that I had surrendered.

CHAPTER SIXTEEN

BEAUTY FROM ASHES

After the judge announced that I would be offered a second chance at life, I wasn't immediately sent home. I had to wait in the county jail until February 6 to be released, but I didn't care. I knew that after those six days, I would be on my way to recovery.

When the day finally came, two women from San Antonio Teen Challenge came to pick me up from the jail. They came in the evening to take me home one last time before it was off to begin my long journey to heal all the wounds I had accumulated over the years. It was absolutely surreal to me that I was leaving those concrete walls behind me for good.

I went through the process of being released. It was like I was being handed my life again; I *was* being handed my life again. I shed my gray canvas skin that read "Inmate" across the back, took off the bracelet that told everyone my life belonged to the State of Texas, and walked out of the jailhouse doors to freedom. As I walked away, I heard something following behind me. It was the sound of applause. I looked back to see the guards and inmates clapping as I walked out of misery and into grace.

The women drove me from the jail to my parents' house. It was a good feeling to finally be sitting in the back of a car without handcuffs and shackles. I wasn't going to take anything for granted anymore, so I stared down at my tiny wrists as we drove and thanked God that they weren't bound my stainless steel cuffs.

We pulled into my driveway, and I couldn't get out of the car fast enough. My family's home looked like something that might be in the second Jerusalem, and I was ready to be inside it with my family. I grabbed my bags and hurried to the front door. If I would have told anyone sixty days earlier that I would be running to my parents' front door, they would have called me a liar. Oh ye of little faith...

My mom saw us drive up and ran out of the house to hug me. When I saw her, I dropped my bags and ran to her in my high heels. I dropped everything in my hands and wrapped my arms around her. It felt so good to be able to hug my mother without a guard watching. We stood like that for quite some time, embracing one another and crying in our front yard.

After we made it through our tearful hellos, we all sat down to have dinner before I had to leave for Teen Challenge. We had to leave for San Antonio that evening, so we didn't have much time, but I was happy to just be able to sit down at a real table with metal silverware and our family dishes I had known my whole life instead of being in a noisy cafeteria with terrible food and people with handguns standing nearby. I was home, and even if it was only for a short time, it was a comfort to me to be there.

After we finished dinner, it was time to pack up and hit the road. My parents went with me on the trip so they could tell me good-bye before I went away to Teen Challenge to learn how to live again.

It was a seven-hour drive from Henderson to San Antonio. As I looked out at the passing cars and over the open fields that seemed to go on forever, I began to get nervous and wonder what was ahead of me. I knew that I was going to have to work really hard on myself and overcome my eating disorder. That was hard for me to process because I could not see my life without it. I had lived with this eating disorder for more than ten years.

I also knew I had to work on all the other issues that had created so many problems in my life. I had always struggled with bitterness, hate, anger, and forgiving those who had hurt me, and it was going to take a lot to overcome that. I knew I also had to stop comparing myself with others. Most importantly, I knew I had to learn to love and accept myself—the real root of my problem. I did not know how to love myself and accept who God made me to be. I had a long road ahead of me, but I was ready, or so I thought.

Finally at 5:00 a.m., we reached Teen Challenge. As we pulled in, I saw a sign at the gate that said "Sin Stops Here." *Yes, it does*, I thought with excited anticipation as we pulled in. I looked ahead and saw the campus that would be my home for the next thirteen months. My parents hugged and kissed me good-bye at the gate because they were not allowed to go any farther. I was overwhelmed with all I was feeling as I said good-bye. I was excited, nervous, overjoyed, and scared. There was so much work to be done to become whole again.

We drove back to a two-story ladies' home in the back of the campus. I walked in and looked around. There were five rooms in the house, each of which had bunk beds in them. The rooms had anywhere from six to ten bunks, so twelve to twenty beds, so I was going to have quite a few roommates. I was fine with that, though. I had been living in a prison with guards watching me shower, so roommates I could handle.

Along with five rooms, there was also a kitchen and living area for everyone to share. Although it wasn't like being home, the place felt warm and comforting, so much so that I immediately put my bags down and slept on a couch in the living area. I was exhausted from all that had happened, so I slept.

After an hour of sleep, I awoke to an intern who greeted me with warmth and open arms. She was so kind and caring; she showed me the love of Jesus from the first moment we met. The intern then began to introduce me to the others. I was overwhelmed by the kindness that each woman showed, both the patients and the staff. It was culture shock after having been in prison.

Because I was the sickest person there, I was cared for more intensely than the others. I came in weighing only eighty-four pounds, and, at first, the staff wasn't quite sure how to treat such a severe case. The staff talked with doctors, though, and came up with a game plan to help me. They were going to have to spend a lot of time with me, but everyone there was more than willing. Where in prison they threw food at me and forced me to eat or let me starve, in Teen Challenge they were determined to find out how to introduce my body to food again so I could become healthy. I was becoming a person again.

As I started my rehabilitation, I realized that the term "born again" applied to me both spiritually and physically. While God worked in me to help give me new eyes to see myself and a new heart to love myself, the staff worked with me to teach me how to live and eat all over again. I was just like an infant in so many ways. I had to learn to live, love, and trust all over again.

My first step to physical recovery was learning to eat. Eating seems like something that should be easy to do, right? Well, not for me. My body had literally forgotten how to. I could not hold food anymore, and forcing me to eat, like they had done in jail, only made things worse. Because of this, I was given an accountability coach and did not eat with the others. I was also put in the care of an amazing woman who worked with me nonstop. She had been to medical school and knew the steps to help me get better.

My recovery was not a fast one. An infant does not learn to walk at two weeks old, and I was no different. Relearning a lifestyle is no easy chore, and it took me and my body time to pick up on the new things that I was learning. I was fed one ounce of food three times a day for several months until I began to improve.

The entire way, I was led by baby steps, moving slowly into new foods and bigger servings. I had been terrified my whole life of gaining weight, so I also had to learn to accept that gaining weight was a necessary part of recovery. For several months I was not able to eat at the table with any of the other ladies because they felt that the sight of food and watching others eat was too hard for me. My caretakers put me in a small room by the kitchen with my accountability partner at meal times. I hated this, and there were many days I just wanted to give up and go back to prison. Many times I tried to leave, but my spirit and strong will wouldn't let me. I just wanted to be normal, and I knew that all this was part of the process to doing that, even if it was extremely difficult.

Overcoming a ten-year battle with bulimia and a lifetime of hurt can be absolutely draining. I found myself turning to God constantly to ask for the strength to carry on. The first few months, I felt like I might be a lost cause. I would pray hard, though, when I felt that way, and God would remind me that I had a calling, that I had not been swallowed up and spit out for no reason. It was a constant struggle to remember that sometimes, though, even with the amazing support around me.

There was a prayer closet in the house that I had been spending a lot of time in my first months at Teen Challenge. One April afternoon when I felt like I had nothing left to give, I walked into that prayer closet and dropped to my knees. Again, I cried out to God. As I sat, weeping and praying, God told me to fast from the mirror and He would give me new eyes. I did just that. For seven days, I did not look into a mirror. I trusted God that He would heal me after my obedience, and He did. After my fast, my rebirth turned into a brand new growing process for me.

Before, every time I looked at myself, it was as if I were looking in a funhouse mirror. My eyes simply refused to see me the way I really was. On the seventh day, I looked in the mirror, and I saw a new person. I saw a new me full of life with a beautiful heart. I saw a beautiful girl with thicker hair, a radiant smile, and eyes full of life—they even turned a different color. God had not only given me a new set of eyes, He gave me a new thought process. Every month I became a little stronger.

Although I still did have battles, my fast led me to victories I never imagined possible. I began to gain weight without anxiety, saw a beauty in me I had never seen before, and I started to change and become healthier. I knew God needed me to overcome my obstacles, and I was bound to do that for Him. I made so much progress in the next couple of months that by month five, I was able to fix my own plate, and I didn't have to have my accountability coach anymore.

In my ninth month, I began to struggle with myself again. I'm not quite sure what came over me, but after five months of gaining weight and eating healthier, I found myself withholding food. I simply did not want to eat, and when I did eat, it was only a tiny amount of food. Clearly, I was experiencing a relapse.

The staff felt I needed help once again. I was back at square one. I had an accountability partner with me through my thirteenth month at Teen Challenge, which seemed heartbreaking at the time but was an actual blessing for me when I needed one. Sometimes we just aren't ready to take the training wheels off, and that is okay.

It was a frustrating and trying time, particularly after all the progress I had made. However, I made up my mind to simply seek God more and press on through the dark days. The more I turned to him, the more real He became. I found the saving power of Jesus Christ through Teen Challenge. Most importantly, I found a deeply intimate relationship with God. I found a loving and forgiving God, one who offered me hope and healing, strength and salvation, deliverance and redemption. He filled my heart with peace and joy and taught me how to love, especially myself. He gave me a reason to live again and gave me people who taught me how.

EPILOGUE

After thirteen months of struggle, I graduated Teen Challenge on March 2, 2010. I had finally completed the long hard road of entering into physical and spiritual recovery. I could not have made it through that sometimes-daunting process if God had not been holding my hand the whole way, never letting go. I am so grateful to the Teen Challenge staff who remained by my side, pushing me to be all that I could be. They saw in me the potential to overcome and win this war against myself. They also used kindness and compassion to change me instead of harshness and hate the way the prisons had. Forty years in prison would have never done for me what thirteen months at Teen Challenge did. Yes, it was hard, and at times I felt that I couldn't do it, but it was well worth it, and because of it, today I am a woman filled with God's love.

After completion of Teen Challenge, I was offered an internship with Shannon Ethridge, best-selling author, international speaker, and certified life coach. Shannon offers a twelve-month mentorship program called B.L.A.S.T. (Building, Authors, Leaders, Speakers, and Teachers) that I completed that provided me the tools I needed to become who I am today and also helped me in the process of starting my own ministry. Among all other things, though, the program has given me a voice of hope, and it has made it possible for God to use me the way He always had planned to.

If you have a passion for speaking or writing, I encourage you to visit Shannon's website and join the B.L.A.S.T. mentorship program. You can go online at www.shannonethridge.com/blast.shtml to find out how.

I am currently traveling and speaking to churches, youth groups, Celebrate Recovery groups, and women's conferences. I am a licensed minister with Church Fellowship International of Henderson, Texas, and I continue to live a life in Christ and am determined to spread the gospel around the world. I am also working on becoming a certified life coach to help coach others through their battles of addiction.

The same year that I completed Teen Challenge, I married Jonathan, the man who was my best friend for many years and the love of my life. Sadly after fourteen months of marriage, we went our separate ways. Although we divorced and weren't a part of one another's live for a short time, God began to work in him, and he has become a part of my life once again. Like I said, there is just something about him that won't let me go. We remarried on June 15, 2012 and have a wonderful relationship. God reconciled us and brought us back to one another. It was all a part of His plan.

God not only reunited me with my amazing husband, but He also brought Elizabeth Layne back into my life again. After all we went through and our time apart, we found each other again at better places in our lives and are best friends today!

As for my eating, I am at a healthy weight now, and I finally feel great, both mentally and physically. I now work out three days a week and have a great desire to be fit and healthy inside and out. I have learned to use my new eyes to see myself and my new heart to love myself, and I am every day becoming stronger in the Lord. It is not an easy process day to day with my eating; I may fall sometimes, but that is where God's grace comes in. Never give up if you fall short; get up and try again. That is what God has taught me in my journey of recovery with this eating disorder.

Now that I have been though hell and come out on the other side, I have a passion to see men and women live in freedom from their hurts, life challenges, and addictions. My life is a living example that anything is possible with God, and I want to use that example to give others hope. I want to use my story to demonstrate to others what strong faith and dedication to the Lord can do. Just like Jonah, now that I have survived the storm and the whale, I want to go out and preach God's love to the people. I have a vision and dream to have a recovery center for women with life-controlling issues—such as eating disorders, drug addiction, alcoholism, sexual abuse, and any other issues that can keep someone in a life of pain and suffering—called Janie's House of Hope. My desire is to help God do for others what He has done for me.

God has placed a great calling on my life to join Him in His work to bring freedom to people everywhere. I spent so much time running away from God, believing that I would find my answers out in the world. Now I know that when God has a plan for your life, you had better listen.

I want you to know God has a plan for your life and He will finish the good work that He has started. Do not be afraid. God has everything in His hands. If He did it for me, then He will do it for you. Trust Him.

I know there are many people reading this that are running from the call of God, just like I was. Wake up and listen to what I am saying. Don't wait until it is too late. Surrender to the call of God, and you will find yourself in a much better place in your life. If you continue to run from God, He will eventually bring you to the place where you will have to choose your way or His. When we choose our own way, we leave an open door for Satan to bring death, destruction, sickness, disease, and addictions into our lives.

Without Christ in our lives, we are empty and full of darkness. I know this and can talk to you this way because I was once where some of you are headed. Stop! There is a way out for you, and His name is Jesus Christ. If you allow Him to, He will take you out of your darkness and bring you into His glorious light! He will fill your life with His peace, joy, and love—even in the midst of trials. He will give you a sense of worth and bring you into a special relationship with Him.

Don't get me wrong—living for Christ is not always easy, but it is rewarding and fulfilling. He takes me to a level that the drugs and alcohol could never do. I must say, at first it is hard to put all your trust in something you cannot see, until the day He allows certain circumstance to arise in your life so that He can manifest Himself and show His awesome power. That is my story! God allowed these circumstances to arise in my life to show me that power, and from that day on I have never been the same. My life has purpose now, and I know what it is. It is to serve the Lord and to bring His message to everyone who is out wandering in the wilderness. I guess it wasn't just my parents after all whom God called so many years ago in Valliant, Oklahoma.

This was me at 14 years old. I was comfort eating and weighed around 200 pounds. We were traveling on the field.

This is me in my world of parties, I.V drugs, alcohol and sex.

This was my Id card for TDC women's prison in February of 2007.

This is me, Mom, and Dad at our visit in the Sky View Unit in Rusk, Texas, the psychiatric ward.

This was in 2008 after prison. My eating disorder was out of control and I was an alcoholic and drug addict. I was 24 years old. I weighed around 90 pounds.

This is my 4th mug shot in Smith County Jail in December of 2008 after I revoked my probation. I was drunk and high.

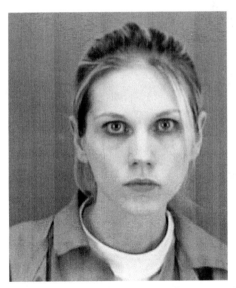

This was my last mug shot in Smith County in January of 2009 after I was bench warranted back from TDC for a new trial. I was very sick and weighed 84 pounds.

After my release from prison on Feb 6, 2009 I took a picture with family on the way to Teen Challenge.

I graduated on March 2, 2010 after a long 13 months in the Teen Challenge program. I went into the program weighing 84 pounds and left the program weighing around 130 pounds.

This one was in 2010 after graduation. So thankful for God's mercy.

Me and my husband Jonathan